"Andrew Abernethy has produced an incredibly accessible and stimulating guide for how to study the Bible. You don't have to be a scholar of Hebrew or Greek, or an expert on ancient Egypt or Rome, as Abernethy shows, all you need is a teachable heart and a desire to learn. If you have that, then Abernethy has a great plan to help you get the most of your study of Holy Scripture, to have your way illuminated by the guiding light of God's Word."

**Michael F. Bird,** academic dean and lecturer in theology at Ridley College in Melbourne, Australia

"*Savoring Scripture* takes seriously the psalmists' confession that the Word of God is rich food that delights and satisfies. Abernethy offers a simple and well-rounded approach to Bible study that opens the path to formation and nourishment. Spiritual reflection without deep study is foolish; study without worship is lifeless. This book intertwines both and makes for a perfect recipe."

**Nijay K. Gupta,** professor of New Testament at Northern Seminary

"We desperately need books that help people in the church read the Bible more faithfully. Andrew Abernethy provides an engaging guide to readers who want to more competently understand this book that has been changing lives for centuries."

**Patrick Schreiner,** associate professor of New Testament and biblical theology at Midwestern Baptist Theological Seminary

"Does the Bible feel intimidating or irrelevant? This step-by-step guide offers a simple but effective way to engage with Scripture for personal transformation. Andrew Abernethy puts his academic credentials in service of the church in this down-to-earth book. Beginners will experience the Bible as was intended—as a true story that changes us and helps us connect with God."

**Carmen Joy Imes,** associate professor of Old Testament at Biola University and author of *Bearing God's Name: Why Sinai Still Matters*

# Savoring
# Scripture

## A Six-Step
## Guide to
## Studying
## the Bible

FOREWORD BY
**Charlie Dates**

## Andrew Abernethy

**ivp**
Academic

An imprint of InterVarsity Press
Downers Grove, Illinois

**InterVarsity Press**
P.O. Box 1400 | Downers Grove, IL 60515-1426
ivpress.com | email@ivpress.com

InterVarsity Press® is the publishing division of InterVarsity Christian Fellowship/USA®. For more information, visit intervarsity.org.

Cover design and image composite: David Fassett
Interior design: Jeanna Wiggins

ISBN 978-1-5140-0409-8 (print) | ISBN 978-1-5140-0410-4 (digital)

Printed in the United States of America ♾

**Library of Congress Cataloging-in-Publication Data**
A catalog record for this book is available from the Library of Congress.

10   9   8   7   6   5   4   3   2   1   |   30   29   28   27   26   25   24   23   22

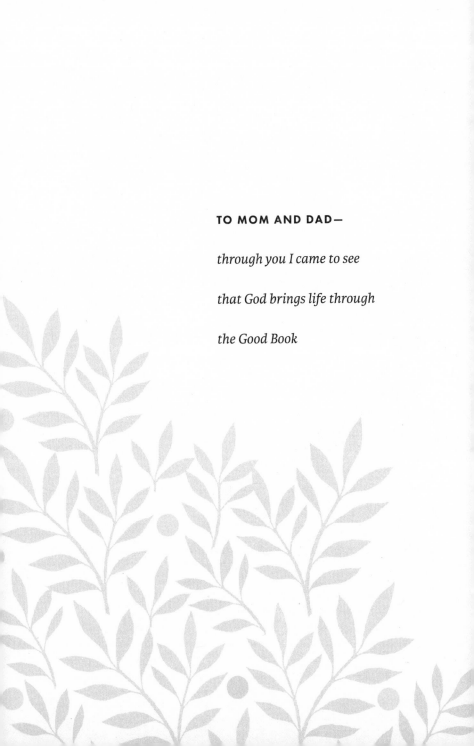

**TO MOM AND DAD—**

*through you I came to see*

*that God brings life through*

*the Good Book*

# Contents

# Foreword

Charlie Dates

WHEN WE WERE STUDENTS AT TRINITY, Andrew Abernethy could hoop! He was one of my favorite guys with whom to play basketball. You could tell his jump shot was polished. His follow-through was poster ready. Despite what the old Wesley Snipes and Woody Harrelson movie said, Andy could jump. So he was joyful competition on the court.

In a season of studying Koine Greek and learning the binyanim of the Masoretic Hebrew text, basketball was a needed outlet. Young seminarians—at least at that time—could be a bit ambitious. The dreams of landing a significant leadership role in the life of the church, some thought, depended on one's academic performance. Too few of us understood that good grades earned in the academy were no guarantee for effectiveness in the church. In seminary, it's easy to confuse exegetical performance with pastoral readiness. In real life, it's also easy to mistake a careful reading of the text with a warm devotional life.

I meet people from time to time who are fascinated with the Old Testament. They want to discern the messages of the prophets and the foreshadowing of Christ in the first covenant. They ask me for people to read, and I send them names like Andrew Abernethy. His is a trusted voice and a wise application. Sometimes people ask Andy for preachers from whom they can listen and learn. And Andy has graciously given them my name.

I want you to recognize that a schooled mind should be close to a blazing heart; that the more informed about God we become, the more in love with God we should be. Sadly, that is not often the case.

What you hold in your hands is a roadmap for both the learning and the burning. It is a compass for direction on how to dig your own wells so that you can drink deeply from the treasures of God's Word. None of us has exhausted the unsearchable riches of God's Word. Not one living human has drained the mind of God for human flourishing. We all need more of God. Every one of us is insatiable until we find the fullness of God in regular devotion.

Do you want that? Do you want more of God? Do you want the substance of things hoped for and the evidence of things not seen? Do you want to understand his ways better? God's Word will give that to you. As a result of reading this book you will have tools to get you there. Andrew can lead the way.

What I especially appreciated about Andrew's game is that he understood basketball. He seemed to intrinsically discern the art of making space between the opponent. He could direct traffic, run screens, and man the post. He was good for the team. I guess it's no surprise that Andrew is a stellar Bible professor. He understands the book, but even better Andrew knows its author.

Life has taught him how to walk with God and lead others to green pastures. You might not be a better basketball player after reading this book, but you will learn to read the Scriptures and consequently love God more. I think that's why you're holding this book now.

# Acknowledgments

I WANT TO RECOGNIZE many who made this book possible. Anna Gissing contracted this book with IVP Academic and believed in this project's vision from the beginning; this gave me confidence to pursue what God had put on my heart for this book. Thanks to my anonymous reviewers, whose suggestions improved this book. Two faculty colleagues at Wheaton College volunteered to offer me feedback on the entire manuscript—Terry Huttenlock, emerita professor of library sciences, and Michael McKoy, associate professor of politics and international relations. I am forever in your debt. My graduate assistant Katie Black offered feedback on every chapter and helped to create the questions at the end of each chapter. Another student, Kendra Gering, worked through every chapter and offered great suggestions. Other colleagues and pastors offered feedback or gave advice on portions of the book: Jordan Ryan, Jim Wilhoit, Heather Zimmerman, Daniel Treier, and Fr. Mathew Woodley. My wife, Katie, offered thoughtful feedback on many of the chapters and, most significantly, continually encouraged me regarding the value of this project. Thank you all for your help and support, but, of course, all deficiencies in this book are my own.

# Prologue

"WHAT DO YOU WANT FOR CHRISTMAS?" I asked my dad a few years ago.

He responded, "How about a book on how to read the Bible?" I was dumbfounded. I couldn't think of one.

My dad turns to me, his son who is a Bible professor, for a book on how to read the Bible that would be just right for him. Yet, I had nothing to recommend.

Here was my dilemma: Some books on how to read the Bible are academically informative, but they can create the sense of a gap between God and us as we read the Bible. Other books are spiritually vibrant, but they provide few valuable tools from academia that can truly help God's people read the Bible better. We need a beginner's guide to Bible study that weds the academic with the spiritual, that integrates textual analysis with the illuminating and transforming work of the Holy Spirit.

In my years teaching, I have seen the same journey repeatedly. A zealous believer wants to learn more about how to read the Bible. They read an academically informed book or receive training at a college or seminary. They come to read the Bible historically, and they are excited about how much more they understand in the Bible.

Gradually, however, the once zealous believer notices a growing gap between themselves and God. Previously they read the Bible with a warm openness to receive from God, but now they read with a cool rationality. Previously they delighted in how God revealed himself and could speak into their present moment, but now they delight in the intellectual satisfaction of arriving at a rational understanding of a passage in its ancient context.

The church is not blind to how academic training can have a cooling effect on the faith. At a Black church on Chicago's South Side, a pastor told his congregation that he would be starting classes at a local seminary. After the service, an elderly woman came up to him with a look of concern. Pointing her finger at him, she said, "Watch out. If you go to seminary, your faith will go to the cemetery."

We need an approach to reading the Bible that will allow our faith to soar rather than sour. We need an approach that can help us draw closer to God rather than away from him. We need an approach to the Bible that recognizes God's ability to speak to us in the moment, in real life, through an ancient book.

The book in your hands (or on your screen) brings together faith and academics. It offers a template for Bible reading that fuels a lively faith and incorporates the academic tools that are most valuable for ordinary Christians. I present to you the six-step approach.

I do not promise that this book will make Bible reading easy. Perhaps God doesn't want it to be easy. *God has given us a Bible that is for the hungry—for those desperate enough to depend on him for provision and who will exert great mental energy or endure seasons of dullness to eventually taste some honey.* My hope is that this book will offer us a strategy for tasting more goodies from God's Word so that we will find nourishment to live faithfully in God's world.

## AT JESUS' FEET

Mary of Bethany is a prime example of one we should strive to be like when it comes to reading God's Word. When Jesus comes to the town of Bethany, he visits Mary's family. According to custom, Mary should be working with her sister Martha in the kitchen, preparing a meal for their honored guest. However, Mary breaks with custom and sits at Jesus' feet, listening to his teaching.

Martha is frustrated: "Lord, don't you care that my sister has left me to do the work by myself? Tell her to help me!" (Lk 10:40). Most likely, Martha would expect Jesus to support her; after all, her sister is shirking responsibility. But Jesus sees Martha as the one who needs correction. Jesus says, "Martha, Martha, you are worried and upset about many things, but few things are needed—or indeed only one. Mary has chosen what is better, and it will not be taken away from her" (Lk 10:41-42). Martha is swept up in the many demands of life and custom, but Mary is fixated on the only thing that is necessary—sitting at Jesus' feet to savor his voice.

Will we learn from Mary? Will we choose what is better? In my own experience, I am often like Martha, even when I read the Bible. I am busy accomplishing tasks as it relates to the Bible. I study, preach, teach, and write about the Bible. Yet, I often fail to sit at the feet of the one who desires to speak through the Bible to me. Mary teaches us to sit at the feet of Jesus as we read his Word.

## MY BACKSTORY

Here is a bit about me. When I was eleven, I first heard the gospel, that Jesus died for my sins. I responded immediately in faith and was filled with the Spirit. By the time I was sixteen, I began to drift. Basketball and partying took over. Night after night I'd ignore the Holy Spirit's conviction and plunge into sin. By the time I turned twenty, I was a borderline alcoholic. I was a Division I athlete whose skills on the court were in sharp decline. I hardly attended class. I received a 0.8 GPA during the first semester of my sophomore year.

God did not give up on me. The Holy Spirit never stopped calling this prodigal son to return to the Father through Christ. I finally turned back to Christ, left behind fraternity life and a Division I scholarship, and transferred to a Christian college.

I had *zero* intention of becoming a pastor, Bible professor, or author when I enrolled at Bethel College in Indiana. I just hoped to get sober and turn my life around. I needed God. Out of this hunger for God I began to read the Bible. It became a lifeline for hearing from God. Those years at Bethel were some of my sweetest times with God in his Word. Eventually, I was called to minister God's Word, went to seminary, pastored for a few years, and then got a PhD. I have now been teaching college and seminary students for over a decade.

Although I now teach the Bible for a living, I have not graduated from my need for the advice given in this book. I remain hungry for God. Depression and anxiety have plagued me since the late 1990s. Since 2010, I have battled a movement disorder called cervical dystonia, forcing me to take refuge in God amid suffering. The Holy Spirit still convicts me of sins—especially those hidden sins of pride, judgmentalism, coveting, and many others. As a result, I remain a beggar, longing for morsels from the Savior. I am not content when reading the Bible becomes merely an academic exercise; I desperately need to meet with the living God every single day. I need the advice in this book as much as anyone else does.

You have your own story, your own journey, that led you to this book. God wants to meet with you through the Bible, so may God use this book for that purpose.

## THE SIX STEPS

We will follow six steps across this book. The term *steps* may have some of you rolling your eyes. I get it. You're skeptical of steps that promise revolution but turn out to be shallow and gimmicky. Let me clarify. These six steps represent longstanding vantage points that God's people have benefited from for thousands of years when reading the Bible. I have put them in an order that make sense to me, but I fully expect that you will find an order and flow that works for you. What is most important to me is to pass along six important vantage points to keep in mind when studying a passage in the Bible.

Here they are:

1. Posture—Orient the beliefs and dispositions of your heart as you prepare to discern God's voice when reading the Bible.

2. Flow—Grasp the flow of thought across a passage in light of its genre and subunits.

3. Context—Ponder the passage in view of its historical setting and its place in its literary context within the biblical book.

4. Whole Bible—Consider how your passage bears witness to Christ and fits into the Bible's redemptive story.

5. Savor God—Ponder, pray to, and praise God in view of who he is revealing himself to be as you go back through the passage.

6. Faithful Response—What is God calling you to do in your life, and in the world, through this passage?

At first, implementing these steps will feel like learning the tango: slow, choppy, and a bit forced. After a season of regular practice, you'll pick up speed, become more fluid, and the steps will become second nature. In my own experience, these "steps" are no longer steps; they are just features of what it means to read the Bible. In the epilogue, I offer some advice about putting these steps into practice. So, if you are wondering whether you can mix up the order or whether you can leave some steps out for time's sake, then feel free to turn to the epilogue at any time.

These steps arise from training students year after year in how to read the Bible. When I first began teaching, my exclusive focus was on passing along the benefits of my academic training. We would focus on finding the flow of thought in a passage in light of its genre (step 2) and the importance of context when reading (step 3). The aim was to listen carefully to what God was saying through the human author to the original audience—recovering a sense of what the passage would have meant originally.

Over time, however, I have seen how too much of a focus on steps two and three can create a wedge between us, God, and the world. The Bible becomes something to figure out, like any ancient historical text. The Bible becomes a word for people back in the day but not for us today.

As important as steps two and three are for Bible reading, they must take their place within the primary purpose of why God has given us his Word—to reveal himself to us, draw us near, speak to us, and transform us. This is where steps one, four, five, and six come into play. Step one describes a disposition of the heart that positions us to hear God's voice. Step four reminds us that any given passage is part of God's grand design that culminates in Jesus. Steps five and six remind us that *the Bible is a means to an end, not the end itself.* The Bible does not exist simply for us to learn stuff. The Bible is a means through which we can hear from God, who invites us through the Word to savor him and to learn how to live today.

## USING THIS BOOK

Before we turn to step one, let me suggest two ways you might use this book.

- Option 1: Read through the entire book to grasp what each step is about and how the steps fit together. Then select a short passage—less than ten verses—and work back through all six steps.

- Option 2: Select a short passage—less than ten verses—right now. As you go through each step, apply what you are learning to your passage before moving on to the next step.

For those interested in using this as part of a group Bible study, see the guidance provided in the epilogue. As you walk through the steps ahead, may the Holy Spirit meet you on the journey, illuminating your heart to savor and respond to God through his Word.

## DISCUSSION QUESTIONS

1. How has God been preparing you to want and benefit from a book like this?

2. Can you describe a time when you longed, like Mary, to simply be with Jesus?

3. What obstacles get in your way of simply being with Jesus?

4. What words come to mind when you think about your past experience of studying the Bible? What has been good about it? What has been hard?

5. *God has given us a Bible that is for the hungry—for those desperate enough to depend on him for provision and who will exert great mental energy to taste some honey.* What words or phrases stick out to you from this sentence, and why? How would you explain this idea in your own words?

*Step 1*

# Posture

I HAD THE CHANCE TO GO TO JERUSALEM in 2014. On the itinerary was "Hezekiah's Tunnel." I was excited to see it. This tunnel under Jerusalem is longer than five football fields. It may have been dug 2,800 years ago when King Hezekiah was preparing to face the Assyrians. On the itinerary, under "Hezekiah's Tunnel," was a caption: "Bring waterproof shoes, a flashlight, and a hat."

It was a dark tunnel with running water, so I knew why I would need my Crocs (yes, grown men can wear Crocs) and a flashlight. But why on earth would I need a hat? Hats are for protecting my eyes or balding scalp from the sun, not for dark tunnels.

As we prepared to enter the tunnel, the leader said, "The ceiling of the tunnel can be as low as five feet in some places, so you'll want to duck down and wear a hat to protect your head from scraping the ceiling." Now I knew why I needed a hat.

I am 6'6". They didn't make tunnels back in ancient times for giants like me. To make it through the tunnel, I had to crouch low and wear a cap for about 500 yards. *Without adopting a lowly posture, there would be no way I'd make it through.*

Similarly, entry into the Bible demands a particular posture of mind and heart. When we read the Bible with the right posture, the odds of meeting with God and hearing his voice increases.

What posture of mind and heart will position us to hear from God as we read the Bible?

## TEACHABILITY

We come to Scripture to meet with God. Don't misunderstand me. I am not saying that we approach the Bible as if it were God— that would be idolatry, *bibliolatry* (worshiping a book rather than the God of the Good Book). Bibliolatry can manifest itself in the innocent guise of wanting to know the Bible. While there is nothing wrong with seeking to study and learn the Bible, bibliolatry surfaces when the quest for knowledge becomes an end in itself.

Jesus confronts some of the most dedicated students of Scripture in ancient Israel. These Jews could have schooled any of us in their knowledge of the Bible. But Jesus was not impressed. He said to them, "You study the Scriptures diligently because you think that in them you have eternal life. These are the very Scriptures that testify about me, yet you refuse to come to me to have life" (Jn 5:39-40).

Scary stuff. It is possible to be the most diligent students of Scripture and still fail Jesus' exam. You fail if your study of Scripture does not lead you to Jesus. What can help us move beyond bibliolatry to encounter God as we read the Bible? The posture of our heart makes a difference. We need to be teachable.

The Bible gives us several vantage points for thinking about teachability. Have you ever thought about our need for God himself to be our teacher? As discussed in the previous chapter, Mary of Bethany models for us a teachable spirit as she sits at the feet of Jesus, hungry for his every word.

This posture before God as teacher includes recognizing our need for God to help us know the things of God. We can't assume that in and of our own efforts we will automatically grasp the Bible.

The psalmist models this. He prays, "Teach me, O Lord, the way of your statutes" (Ps 119:33 ESV). No doubt the psalmist had studied God's statutes, but he knew that for them to sink in God would need to teach him. The prophets themselves look forward to a time when God would teach his people (Is 30:20-21; Jer 31:34). Jesus even speaks to his disciples about how the Holy Spirit would teach his disciples (Jn 14:26). As we approach the Bible, then, we need to come with hearts yearning to be taught by God, the Master Teacher himself.

## CHILDLIKENESS

Another vantage point on teachability is childlikeness. We are coming to meet with God, our Father, when we approach the Scriptures. Jesus highlights childlikeness as a key to hearing God's voice. Consider this scenario in Matthew 11.

Jesus is traveling from city to city around the Sea of Galilee. Miracles are happening left and right. With just a touch, Jesus cleanses a leper, relieves the fever of Peter's mother-in-law, and opens the eyes of the blind. With just a word, Jesus heals a paralyzed servant and casts out a legion of demons. People from across the region are bringing the sick and demon possessed before him, and they are all experiencing healing and deliverance.

If you witnessed such events, how would you respond? You'd repent and turn to Jesus, right? Well, maybe not. Check out what Matthew says: "Jesus began to denounce the towns in which most of his miracles had been performed, because they did not repent" (Mt 11:20). Those who saw the mighty works of God in their midst were calloused, unchanged, and unresponsive. So Jesus curses those cities, declaring that Sodom is better off than them. This is not good news, considering the fact that God wiped Sodom off the map due to their sin in Genesis 19.

Jesus next says something that seems like it is out of left field: "I praise you, Father, Lord of heaven and earth, because you have hidden these things from the wise and learned, and revealed them to little children. Yes, Father, for this is what you were pleased to do" (Mt 11:25-26). Hold on a minute. Jesus was just calling down curses, and now he's praising God. What is going on? What is happening becomes clear when we see the contrast between Jesus condemning the "wise and learned" *who do not get it* (the cities of Galilee who remain unrepentant after seeing miracles) and those "little children" *who do get it*.

The ways of the Father are far different from what one would expect. From a human point of view, the "wise and learned" of Jesus' day—those scribes and Pharisees who went to "seminary"—are those you would expect to grasp the things of God, to repent on seeing God's miracles in Jesus. There is nothing wrong with being "wise" per se. The issue is their assumption that their status in society as those in the know gives them the inside track on knowing the ways of God. They have God in a box, so they are closed off to being pushed beyond their current thinking about God. Jesus takes great delight in how the Father hides these things from the proud who presume a privileged place of being in the know.

Who are the "little children" that receive God's unexpected revelation? Jesus does not have in mind *actual* infants; instead, "little children" is a metaphor for Jesus' disciples. Jesus speaks of his disciples as "little ones" (Mt 10:42) or as "the least" (Mt 11:11) right before this.

One reason why Jesus speaks of his disciples as little children is because infants are not known for their intelligence. If you spend time around little children you know this.

My son Oliver is two as I write this book. The following conversation is typical.

"Oliver, how old are you?"

"Five," he'll declare.

"No, Oliver, you are two," I respond.

"Two," he'll echo back.

So, I follow up by asking: "Oliver, how old are you?"

"Five," he announces with pride.

We get lots of laughs about this. My son amazes me. I love him to bits. But he—along with all other little children—are not intellectually developed, so they are not known to be the "wise and learned" in society.

When Jesus celebrates how "infants" are recipients of divine revelation, he taps into the common knowledge that little children are not expected to be smarter about the ways of God than schooled scribes. Jesus is celebrating how the Father reveals himself to those who might not be "wise and learned" in the world's eyes. Jesus calls fishermen, tax collectors, prostitutes, and the lowly to receive insight into the ways of God in Jesus. These are the "little children." The key seems to be that such folks would not presume to be in the know when it comes to the things of God. This creates a childlike dependence on God for him to make himself known to them. They are open, teachable. Childlikeness seems to be the key, and, as Jesus says elsewhere, we must become like children to enter the kingdom of God (Mt 18:3). The very posture that enables us to enter the kingdom is the posture that positions us to hear from God as we read the Bible.

## WHERE DO YOU FIT?

Would you be among the "wise and learned"—those whom people would expect to understand the things of God due to status and training? Are you a Bible quiz champ, Sunday school teacher, Christian school kid, Bible major, pastor, or a professor? Well, here's a warning. Having a status as "one who knows the Bible" could become a barrier between you and God if this has led to pride and presumption, for the Father takes pleasure in hiding things from folks like us.

Would you be among the "little children"? Some of you may feel like you'd be the last person to receive insight into the things of God. You don't have formal training in how to read the Bible. You didn't get good grades in school. You've made choices in life that have brought you to rock bottom. The Father takes great pleasure in making you the sort of person that will receive his revelation.

As I shared in the prologue, I began studying the Bible as one of the "little children" at the age of twenty. I had a 0.8 GPA, was untangling from substance abuse and deeply depressed, and was definitely not someone people would peg as one who'd grasp the things of God. But I'll tell you what. It was there, amidst my desperation, where God took delight in revealing himself to me through his Word. The floodgates opened and divine wisdom and insight poured through the Scriptures into my barren heart and mind.

I now find myself among the wise and learned. I have degrees. I teach the Bible for a living. I am invited to speak on podcasts and at churches. I write about the Bible. Honestly, my teachability waxes and wanes. I can read and interpret a passage of the Bible to get an A+, but some days and some seasons it seems like the floodgates of divine revelation have been closed. I too often turn on autopilot and just let my training kick in to accomplish the task of interpretation. Thankfully, God does not leave me there. God will allow a thirst, a hunger, a yearning to swell within my unwell soul. Desperation for the things of God will overcome me, and I again become childlike, dependent on God to feed me and help me truly see. Sure, I benefit from my training, but the gates of revelation open when I reach the point of *depending* completely on God and not my status or training.

The apostle Paul gives someone like me hope. Paul was a Pharisee of Pharisees. He was wise and learned, and such learning led him to reject Christianity and persecute Christians. But then God knocked him off of his high horse. His scales of pride and presumed understanding fell from his eyes, and then he could see. There is no doubt Paul continued to benefit greatly from his prior educational training, but Paul no longer leaned on such learning as a sure indication that he had figured out God and his Word.

Paul says this: "No one knows the thoughts of God except the Spirit of God. What we have received is not the spirit of the world, but the Spirit who is from God, so that we may understand what God has freely given us" (1 Cor 2:11-12). Paul knew firsthand that the Spirit of God is the only way we can understand God. We desperately need the Holy Spirit. In steps five and six, we will explore further how the Holy Spirit illuminates our minds to see Christ, personalizes God's Word to the specifics of our lives, and transforms us into people who can respond faithfully to God's Word.

When we come to Scripture, we must come with the posture of an infant—the posture that nothing about our status or intellect is a guarantee we'll hear from God. We don't have God figured out. We come dependent on the Master Teacher and Father to reveal himself to us.

## ADOPTION

Yes, Jesus speaks of his disciples as "little children" to highlight how unexpected it is that they are the recipients of divine revelation. There is another reason why he calls his disciples "little children." They are not just childlike; they are actually God's children.

Did you notice how Jesus starts these verses off by saying, "I praise you Father, Lord of heaven and earth" (Mt 11:25)? The very ruler of everything—heaven and earth—is addressed as Father. It is the Father who hides and reveals. Jesus views the disciples as little children because they have such a unique relationship to God as Father.

Is coming to God as Father part of your DNA? When I was a junior in college, a mentor gave me J. I. Packer's *Knowing God*. In his chapter "Adoption," one sentence jumped out at me: "If you want to judge how well a person understands Christianity, find out how much he makes of the thought of being God's child, and having God as his Father."[1] This was a jaw dropping moment for me. I had never let the truth of God being my Father settle in. Certainly, if someone were to judge my understanding of Christianity based on this, I would have failed.

My tendency is to create God into some sort of cosmic coach. He's given me a spot on the team, so I need to work hard, grind it out through practice, try to perform well, and hope that the coach is happy with how I've done. This god of my own creation is not the God of the Bible, and this mentality leads to a constant sense that I'm not bringing enough to the table. As we've seen, though, an "infant" mentality is one of complete dependence. It is not about what we have to offer; instead, it is about the Father's love in adopting us and about what he wishes to offer us. Thanks be to God that we can relate with him as a child to a Father, not as a player to a coach. Our Father sent Jesus so that we can be adopted as God's children.

Look at how Jesus finishes this passage in Matthew 11:26: "Yes, Father, for this is what you were pleased to do." Let "pleased" sink in. The Father doesn't grudgingly hide things from the wise and reveal things to his children. It is the very pleasure of the Father to work in this way, to make himself known to the lowly, to children like you and me.

---

[1] J. I. Packer, *Knowing God* (1973; repr., Downers Grove, IL: InterVarsity Press, 1993), 201.

This truth must infuse our outlook as we approach the Bible. Our posture should be "Father, as your child, I depend on you to help me see!" And, if Jesus is correct, then the Father is delighted to reveal himself to us, his children.

## TRUST

If childlikeness should be a key posture when we come to Scripture, two features spring from it: trust and family. Let's begin with trust. Children depend on others for just about everything, so they have to trust those around them, especially their family. This same characteristic of childlike trust is vital for our relationship with God as we read his Word.

"Do you trust me?" Aladdin asks Princess Jasmine this twice. In one scene, street boy Aladdin helps Jasmine escape from those hunting her down in the market. As the street boy and princess scramble away across rooftops, they reach a point where they will need to jump. Jasmine is scared, but Aladdin says, "Do you trust me?" After internalizing this question, she jumps.

In a later scene, Aladdin is disguised as Prince Ali. He offers the princess a ride on his magic carpet. She says, "Is it safe?" He responds, "Sure, do you trust me? . . . Do you trust me?" These words cause her to flash back to the marketplace, and then she smiles, says yes, takes his hand, and steps onto the magic carpet.

As we approach the Bible, we should hear the words: "Do you trust me?" Yet, these words do not come to us from a resourceful kid like Aladdin. These words come to us from our heavenly Father. God wants us, his children, to trust him as we come to his Word.

Fundamental to this trust is confidence that Genesis through Revelation is the inspired Word of God. Paul's letter to Timothy supports this: "All Scripture is God-breathed and is useful for teaching, rebuking, correcting and training in righteousness, so that the servant of God may be thoroughly equipped for every good work" (2 Tim 3:16-17). When Paul says, "All Scripture," he has the Old Testament in mind. There was no New Testament at the time of Paul. But if Paul affirms that God inspired the Scriptures throughout Israel's history, we can expect that God would also inspire a new collection of writings to speak of Jesus, the culminating act in God's plan. These Scriptures are "God-breathed," for the very life-giving breath of God that created the world also gave birth to these words. One implication of this is that we should come to the Scriptures trusting that they come from our good Father and that they will be for our good.

This posture toward the Bible is much different from what we see in society. It is often *suspicion*, not trust, that drives some approaches to the Bible. Richard Dawkins and other New Atheists have made it their aim to undermine the Bible. Many modern Bible scholars treat the Bible like any other ancient document and criticize its supernatural claims. Suspicions about the Bible circulate around society, so most who have never read the Bible are already suspicious. Today, some well-meaning Christians will also be suspicious of elements in the Bible that rub them the wrong way. Then they'll discard such passages as problematic.

If our heavenly Father has given us a book that bears his very words, we should receive it as children with trust. This does not mean, however, that we won't have questions. Our heavenly

Father is big enough for us to ask the hardest of questions. I remember some useful advice from one of my theology professors. He said, "When you find a passage in the Bible that rubs you the wrong way, mark that passage so that you can come back to it. It could be that God may want to expand your view of him through that passage."

Esau McCaulley captures this posture of trust well. Instead of dismissing the Bible when something difficult emerges, he says, "I propose . . . that we adopt the posture of Jacob and refuse to let go of the text until it blesses us."[2] What a wonderful posture of trust!

## FAMILY

In addition to trust, valuing family should spring from a child-like posture. I'm not talking about valuing your biological family (though you should value them too!). I'm talking about God's family, including God's children from across all times, generations, and cultures.

Being part of God's family should help us see that our own vantage point is limited. We need the insights of our sisters and brothers and spiritual fathers and mothers to understand God's Word and see what we might be missing. Here are a few examples of this.

My expertise is in Isaiah, so I have preached, taught, and written on one of its most famous passages, Isaiah 6. This is when Isaiah has a vision of God and says, "In the year king Uzziah died, I saw the Lord seated on the throne, high and exalted." I had

---

[2]Esau McCaulley, *Reading While Black: African American Biblical Interpretation as an Exercise in Hope* (Downers Grove, IL: IVP Academic, 2020), 21.

never, however, thought to ask how it is possible for Isaiah, who is human, to see God, who is spirit, until I read Thomas Aquinas's (1200s) commentary on Isaiah. Aquinas's interests expanded my horizon to ponder the wonders of how it would be possible for a human to see God.

*Reception history* explores how biblical texts have been received and interpreted in writing, art, and music in various cultures and across history.

Another example. I had been teaching Ruth for years in the pulpit and classroom, in English and in Hebrew. I felt like I had a great grasp of its message—that was until I heard my colleague Dr. M. Daniel Carroll R. say, "I don't know how anyone can possibly read Ruth or Esther and not think about immigration."

Honestly, I hadn't connected the dots before. All of a sudden, tons of aspects in Ruth came into view simply by being alert to immigration. You see, Danny is not only a brilliant scholar, but he is half Guatemalan and spent many years living in Guatemala. He could see things I could not because of his life experiences.

Another example comes from a conversation with the Rev. Dr. Charlie Dates. A simple observation from Pastor Dates helped to explode a false dichotomy. He said, "We [the Black Church] are far more conservative and orthodox theologically than the White Church. But when people see us involved in social issues they assume we are liberal theologically. Here's the thing, Andy: we haven't had the luxury of separating our pursuit of pure doctrine from the urgent need for social action." All of a sudden I could see how my own context's focus on reading the Bible for right doctrine had caused us to miss the Bible's corresponding interest in social action. The two aren't mutually exclusive! Hearing Pastor Dates's perspective helped to widen my understanding of Scripture. The more alert we are to the perspectives of brothers and sisters in our family the more we will be able to hear the fullness of what God's Word is communicating.

God gave us a Bible that is best read with others. If you've been in a group Bible study, you can attest to this. This is iron sharpening iron. It is like a team of doctors at Mayo Clinic coming together to see the whole picture. When we welcome and value the perspectives and voices of others, we are valuing the family of God. We become childlike and abandon any inclination of self-sufficiency. We depend on God and benefit from our family. As a result, we hear God's voice more clearly.

*Family questions.* What does it look like practically to benefit from the insights of others? It is unrealistic to think we will always have a diverse range of vantage points immediately available to us every time we read the Bible. A fruitful way forward is to become alert to the sorts of questions our brothers and sisters might ask when reading the Bible.

Asian and African communities teach other communities to ask, "How is honor and shame at work in this passage?" and, "Is there a focus on the community or the individual in this passage?" It is so easy for me to overlook how the prodigal son shamed his father and entire family when asking for his inheritance, but a reader from an Asian culture would easily recognize this element of bringing shame on one's family that animates the passage. Whereas Ruth is often depicted as a love story between Ruth and Boaz in White circles, African and Asian readers will be more likely to see that the book is really about God's preservation of a family and the restoration of its honor.

African American and Hispanic communities teach other communities to ask, "How might this passage speak to the plights of the marginalized today?" Esau McCaulley calls this the "Black ecclesial instinct,"[3] and he models this by pondering Scripture in conversation with topics such as policing, slavery, injustice, and Black identity. Justo L. González calls this reading with "Hispanic eyes," and he draws on the Bible to ponder God's plan for the marginalized, the poor, and immigrants.[4]

White and European communities primarily ask, "What doctrine does this teach?" or, "How might this passage have been understood in its ancient context?" These too are valuable questions.

Although these examples relate to cultural groups, we could expand the circle to pretty much anyone else. I've benefited from reading folks of different colors, genders, nationalities, age ranges, and economic statuses. In fact, pretty much anyone we read with could help us see aspects of the Bible we might overlook.

In the previous chapter, I stated, *God has given us a Bible that is for the hungry—for those desperate enough to depend on him for provision and who will exert great mental energy to taste some honey.* We can now add that the Bible God gave us is best read with *all* of our sisters and brothers.

---

[3]McCaulley, *Reading While Black*, 19, 165.
[4]Justo L. González, *Santa Biblia: The Bible Through Hispanic Eyes* (Nashville: Abingdon, 1996).

## CONCLUSION

By way of conclusion, let's go back to where step one started: Jerusalem. All 6'6" of me made it through Hezekiah's Tunnel. I crouched low and wore a hat. The posture helped, but without a flashlight the journey would have been nearly impossible. It is the same when reading the Bible.

Just like my crouching and wearing the hat through the tunnel, encountering the Bible like a child is essential! Yet without the shining light of the Holy Spirit our hearts will remain dull. Jesus tells us that God will provide the Holy Spirit if we ask him (Lk 11:13).

As we enter our time of Bible reading, we need to begin by considering our posture before God. We come as children, dependent on God. The church through the ages has produced countless prayers and songs that you might want to use as you begin to study the Bible. You can also create your own. Here's is a prayer you might adopt: "Our Father, we come as your children. We long to sit at your feet and hear your voice. Send your Holy Spirit that we might savor the Son as we read your word. We are hungry for you. Speak, O Lord. In the name of your Son, Jesus Christ. Amen."

## DISCUSSION QUESTIONS

1. Do you currently identify more with the "wise and learned" or with the "little children"? Why?

2. What does it take to cultivate a spirit of childlikeness?

3. What does it reveal about the character of God that he delights in revealing himself to "little children"?

4. What causes a posture of suspicion when it comes to the Bible? What difference would having a posture of trust make when reading the Bible?

5. Who are the main teachers, pastors, theologians, or authors from whom you learn about Scripture? How many of them are ethnically or culturally different from you? What can we gain in our understanding of Scripture from listening to diverse voices from within the family of God?

6. Write your own prayer that reflects a childlike posture that you can use when beginning to study God's Word.

If you would like to benefit from the insights of the global church as you read the Bible, consider getting either the *Africa Bible Commentary* (Zondervan, 2010) or the *South Asia Bible Commentary* (Zondervan, 2015). You might also like Esau McCaulley's *Reading While Black* (IVP Academic, 2020) and Justo González's *Santa Biblia* (Abingdon, 1996).

*Step 2*

# Flow

GOD HAS GIVEN US A BIBLE with a *flow*. God invites us into a flow of thought he inspired human authors to convey. In this flow, you will come to see what the author intended to communicate in the passage. Once we detect the flow of thought across a passage we can better grasp what God has inspired the author to communicate.

When I think *flow*, I think *Hamilton*. *Hamilton* is the Broadway musical that intertwines hip-hop and rap to depict the life of Alexander Hamilton, a founding father of America. When I first listened to the soundtrack, I couldn't grasp the lyrics. I was just hearing words and lines isolated from one another. But I kept listening. I then saw *Hamilton* in theater and then on Disney+. Eventually, word connected to word, line to line, and I found the flow.

> I am not throwin' away my shot
> Hey, yo, I'm just like my country
> I'm young, scrappy, and hungry
> And I'm not throwin' away my shot.

Alexander Hamilton is an orphan who saw a chance to climb the ladder and impact the founding of America, so he went for it—he didn't throw away his shot. Like America, Hamilton is young, scrappy, and hungry. He's going to go for it. These lyrics finally made sense to me when I found the flow from one line to the next.

I see flow when my wife, Katie, performs the violin. When she is learning a new piece, Katie says, "I need to get this into my fingers." Slowly and deliberately she masters note after note. Then note links to note, measure to measure, and then finally a song with beautiful flow sounds forth.

Just as finding the flow of songs can take time, so also does finding the flow across a passage of the Bible. When we find it, the seemingly isolated and disconnected verses click into place and we understand what a passage is trying to communicate. Step two gives guidance on how to grasp the flow of thought across a passage.

## FOCUS AND DISTRACTION

One challenge when trying to read Bible passages is that we are so easily distracted. Can you relate to the following scenario? You're finally alone in your room. You crave fellowship with God. You pray along the lines of step one, and then open the Bible to John 1. Then the battle begins.

"In the beginning was the Word . . ."

*I wonder if I have any likes on my latest Instagram post.*

"and the Word was with God."

*Wait, did I have the date wrong for my test? Let me check my syllabus.*

"And the Word was God."

*I can't believe there is another report of abuse in the church.*

*Did my phone just ding?*

*Oh! Lord, have mercy! I can't focus right now.*

Ever had a similar experience of a drifting mind when reading the Bible? This is not a sign that you are unspiritual. It is truly hard to get our brains to focus and find the flow of a passage.

> *Exegesis* is the analysis of a biblical text with the aim of grasping what an original author intended to convey to an original audience.
> Steps two and three are fundamental to exegesis.

Have you ever wondered why God doesn't just download the Bible from his GodCloud onto our cranial hard drives? This would certainly make life easier! But remember, God has *given us a Bible that is for the hungry—for those desperate enough to depend on him for provision and who will exert great mental energy to taste some honey.*

Sometimes what we need is to become more *active* in the reading process. Then our brains and hearts can focus on detecting God's voice across the flow of a passage. This chapter will revolve around two tips to help you become more active as you look for the *flow* in a passage—identifying subunits and being sensitive to genre.

## SUBUNITS, SUBUNITS, SUBUNITS

Subunits. There is nothing flashy about the name, but my students regularly report that finding subunits is the key that unlocks the passage's flow for them.

What is a subunit? If we think of our whole passage as a *unit*, then *subunits* are the smaller parts of the whole passage. Once you figure out what the parts are then you can better detect how they relate together to make a whole.

In order to find subunits, we must start by figuring out where a passage begins and ends. To identify a passage, look for significant shifts from one episode to another or from one major thought to the next. Sometimes a chapter of the Bible constitutes a passage. For instance, in 1 Samuel 17, the entire chapter recounts the episode of David and Goliath. Other times there can be multiple passages within a chapter. In 1 Samuel 16, there are two passages, first regarding David's election as king (1 Sam 16:1-13) and second, David's role in serving King Saul (1 Sam 16:14-23). So, before looking for subunits, we should have a sense for where our passage begins and ends.

Now it is time to identify and track our subunits. I will illustrate the process of finding subunits through reference to Psalm 121 (see fig. 2.1).

Begin by *reading the passage* for important initial exposure.

Next, *identify the subunits of thought*. Going slowly through the passage, put a slash (/) where you notice a significant shift from one thought to the next. Has the passage shifted to a new topic? Is there a change in tone? If you are reading a narrative, has there been a shift from one scene to the next? If you are reading poetry, is there a shift to a new set of metaphors or new topic? Sure, you could put a slash after every clause and end up with ten subunits, but think bigger, across multiple verses.

Psalm 121:1 and Psalm 121:2 both use the word *help*, so it is reasonable to see Psalm 121:1-2 as the first subunit. A new topic pertaining to "sleep" occurs across Psalm 121:3-4. A new array of imagery revolving around "shade" occurs across Psalm 121:5-6. Finally, there seems to be a summary statement of confidence in Psalm 121:7-8. So, the slash marks suggest shifts in thought from Psalm 121:1-2, 3-4, 5-6, 7-8. These are my subunits.

After putting in slashes, *look for repeated or related ideas and terms* across the entire passage. Create a code for identifying these associations. So, I double-underline the repeated term "watches," small dash underline mentions of "the LORD," and more. This coding system helps me easily see repeated words or ideas within each subunit and also across the whole.

## Tracking Subunits

Much of my advice pertains to your physically marking the biblical text. If you do not want to write in your Bible, here are some other options:

*Print* out the passage, as I commonly do for my students when I have them actively engage the text.

*Scripture journals* are becoming increasingly common among my students. The NET and ESV publish "Scripture journals" of individual books of the Bible. These provide a blank page next to each page of text from the Bible.

*Six-Step Template.* In appendix two, I provide a template for how you might take notes in your own journal as you read a passage from the six different steps spelled out in this book.

*Careful reading.* If you are antimarking, don't journal, or don't have a pencil handy, much of the advice below can be implemented through a careful reading and rereading. My wife tells her violin students to go over their piece five times each time they practice. Repetition with your mind attuned to the advice in step two will help you better grasp the flow even without marking.

Now, *write a title for each subunit*. As you write these, use ideas or words you see in that subunit. Write these in the margin next to the subunit of text. Usually, you will only need four to ten words for each summary or title, but if you need more that is fine. The goal is to get you to actively process what each subunit is saying.

Finally, read carefully back through Psalm 121, listening for how the thoughts flow from one subunit to the next. I might even craft a summary sentence for the whole, such as this: "An expression of confidence that God is our helper and watcher because he made the world, never sleeps, and is our protective shade."

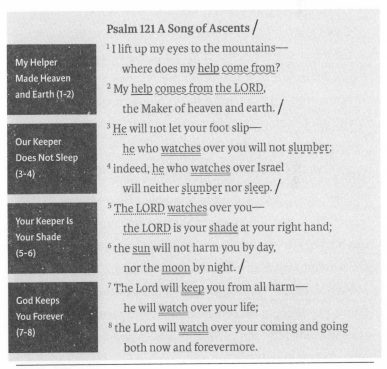

My Helper
Made Heaven
and Earth (1-2)

Our Keeper
Does Not Sleep
(3-4)

Your Keeper Is
Your Shade
(5-6)

God Keeps
You Forever
(7-8)

Psalm 121 A Song of Ascents /
¹ I lift up my eyes to the mountains—
　　where does my <u>help</u> <u>come from</u>?
² My <u>help</u> <u>comes from</u> the LORD,
　　the Maker of heaven and earth. /
³ <u>He</u> will not let your foot slip—
　　<u>he</u> who <u>watches</u> over you will not <u>slumber</u>;
⁴ indeed, <u>he</u> who <u>watches</u> over Israel
　　will neither <u>slumber</u> nor <u>sleep</u>. /
⁵ The <u>LORD</u> <u>watches</u> over you—
　　the <u>LORD</u> is your <u>shade</u> at your right hand;
⁶ the <u>sun</u> will not harm you by day,
　　nor the <u>moon</u> by night. /
⁷ The Lord will <u>keep</u> you from all harm—
　　he will <u>watch</u> over your life;
⁸ the Lord will <u>watch</u> over your coming and going
　　both now and forevermore.

**Figure 2.1.** Text of Psalm 121

Now it's your turn. Let's use Ephesians 2:1-10 as an example. Begin with reading the passage.

[1]As for you, you were dead in your transgressions and sins, [2]in which you used to live when you followed the ways of this world and of the ruler of the kingdom of the air, the spirit who is now at work in those who are disobedient.[3]All of us also lived among them at one time, gratifying the cravings of our flesh and following its desires and thoughts. Like the rest, we were by nature deserving of wrath. [4]But because of his great love for us, God, who is rich in mercy, [5]made us alive with Christ even when we were dead in transgressions—it is by grace you have been saved. [6]And God raised us up with Christ and seated us with him in the heavenly realms in Christ Jesus, [7]in order that in the coming ages he might show the incomparable riches of his grace, expressed in his kindness to us in Christ Jesus. [8]For it is by grace you have been saved, through faith—and this is not from yourselves, it is the gift of God—[9]not by works, so that no one can boast. [10]For we are God's handiwork, created in Christ Jesus to do good works, which God prepared in advance for us to do.

Now *identify the subunits of thought* by putting a slash (/) where you notice a significant shift from one thought to the next. (Do not peek at my work in figure 2.2; it is essential for you to do the work of wrestling with the text yourself.)

Next, *look for repeated or related ideas and terms* across the entire passage. Create a code for identifying these associations. Go ahead and have fun coding your passage around repeated or related ideas and words.

Now attempt to *write a title for each subunit.*

Finally, read back slowly through your passage listening for its flow, drawing on step one: "Father, speak to me, your child."

You might even try to write a summary sentence that encapsulates the entire passage (all subunits should be reflected in the summary statement).

So, how did it go? Did actively marking and writing help you to focus? Did finding subunits help some light bulbs turn on? My hope is that your grasp of the entire passage and its flow has improved dramatically.

Figure 2.2 shows what I have come up with for Ephesians 2:1-10. It is almost certain that our work will differ. I probably missed some things, and I might have noticed some things you missed. Keep in mind that Paul may not have one exact structure of subunits in mind. Identifying subunits is an exercise for *us* to help us enter the flow of the passage.

My subunits are Ephesians 2:1-3, 4-7, 8-10. The tone shifts from negative to positive between Ephesians 2:3 and Ephesians 2:4—it all hinges on God's great love! Although Ephesians 2:4-10 are all positive, there seems to be a focus on the topic of works in Ephesians 2:8-10 that is not in focus in Ephesians 2:4-7.

The layers of repetition show us so many insights across these subunits. It is striking how different Ephesians 2:1-3 is to Ephesians 2:4-10. The first subunit contains none of the gems of the rest of the passage: Christ Jesus, grace, love, salvation, and God's riches. Without God's loving, gracious salvation in Jesus, the destiny of the dead is wrath. Imagine the passage ending after Ephesians 2:3!

The main connection between Ephesians 2:1-3 and Ephesians 2:4-7 is "dead in transgressions." It occurs in Ephesians 2:1 and in Ephesians 2:5. If the flow hinges on God's love, the overarching movement in the passage is from death to life—through

Christ—due to God's love. God has lovingly made dead sinners alive and raised us up in Christ.

| | Ephesians 2 |
|---|---|
| **All Dead in Sinful Course of the World (1-3)** | As for you, you were <u>dead in your transgressions and sins</u>, [2]in which you used to live when you followed <u>the ways of this world and of the ruler of the kingdom of the air, the spirit who is now at work in those who are disobedient</u>. [3]All of *us* also lived among them at one time, gratifying the <u>cravings of our flesh</u> and following its desires and thoughts. Like the rest, *we* were by nature deserving of wrath. / |
| **In Love and Grace, God Made Us Alive in Christ (4-7)** | [4]But because of his <u>great love</u> for *us*, God, who is <u>rich in mercy</u>, [5]made us <u>alive</u> with <u>Christ</u> even when *we* were <u>dead in transgressions</u>— <u>it is by grace you have been saved</u>. [6]And God raised us up with <u>Christ</u> and seated *us* with him in the heavenly realms <u>in Christ Jesus</u>, [7]in order that in the coming ages he might show the incomparable <u>riches of his grace</u>, expressed in his <u>kindness</u> to *us* <u>in Christ Jesus</u>. / |
| **Saved by Grace (Not Works) for Good Works (8-10)** | [8]For <u>it is by grace you have been saved</u>, through faith—and this is not from yourselves, <u>it is the gift of God</u>—[9]not by <u>works</u>, so that no one can boast. [10]For *we* are God's handiwork, created <u>in Christ Jesus</u> to <u>do good works</u>, which God prepared in advance for *us* to do. |

**Figure 2.2.** Text of Ephesians 2:1-10

One final observation from the repetition. Ephesians 2:4-7 and Ephesians 2:8-10 both contain "by grace you have been saved," but only verses Ephesians 2:8-10 mention "works" (twice). This indicates that verses Ephesians 2:8-10 clarify how works relate to being saved by grace. Our works are unable to save us, but God has graciously saved us in Christ to do good works.

> *Word study* is an investigation into the various meanings of a word in its ancient context to clarify what a word means within the flow of a passage. See appendix one for guidance.

As one attends to the repetition across a passage, particular repeated words might invite further investigation. Since it is easy to go wrong with "word studies," I've held off on offering guidance on how to do a word study until appendix one.

The flow of thought begins to come into view by uncovering subunits and repetition across these subunits: *We were dead in our sinful course of life, but God graciously made us alive in Christ to give us a new way in life, one of doing good works.* Identifying subunits can be a key for unlocking the flow of thought across a passage.

## GENRE, GENRE, GENRE

Genre. It is a term many know from music. When you log into Spotify, music options are arranged into genre. We instinctively know what genre we are listening to and how that genre works—you know its typical outlook on life, its rhythm and pacing, and even the sorts of instruments to expect. It is the same with literature. When you read a novel like *The Hobbit*, you know it is a fictional tale; you don't read it as if it were an actual account of New Zealand's history. When you read an Instagram post, you know it is a quick snapshot into someone's life at a particular moment; you don't read the post like you would a biography. We seamlessly move from one genre to the next, knowing exactly what to expect from and what to draw out of a text in light of its genre.

God's playlist in the Bible also has a wide mix of genres: genealogies, narratives, laws, songs, proverbs, prophecy, apocalyptic, Gospels (biography), parables, and letters. Yet, as we move from track to track, interpreting these genres doesn't feel as natural. We often feel lost because these ancient genres are unfamiliar to us.

Being alert to a passage's genre will contribute to detecting its flow. Genre is something you can be mindful of as you take the steps above to figure out a passage's subunits. Here is some advice for reading four of the Bible's most common genres: narrative, poetry, law, and letter.

*Narrative.* Narrative is another word for story. Narratives invite us to see our lives as part of an unfolding plot where God is at work carrying out his purposes. Passages in the following books from the Old Testament are mostly in the narrative genre: Genesis, Exodus, Numbers, Joshua, Judges, Ruth, 1–2 Samuel, 1–2 Kings, 1–2 Chronicles, Ezra, Nehemiah, Esther, Daniel, and Jonah. In the New Testament, the Gospels (Matthew, Mark, Luke, and John) and Acts are narratives too—they are biographies of Jesus and the early church. Narrative is the most common genre in the Bible.

I will use Genesis 12:10-20 as an example of narrative because it is short and raises some interesting questions we'll return to in steps three and four. Here are two tips for reading narrative.[1]

---

[1] Elements of narrative like "setting" and the larger narrative a passage is part of will be dealt with in "Step 3: Context."

*Look for the plot in the narrative.* A plot is a chain of events where a conflict eventually reaches a climax, then dies down, and finds resolution. If you can figure out what the conflict is, then you have a good grasp of what animates the story and its central focus.

There are two fundamental elements to look for to discover the plot: (1) how the scenes relate to one another and, related, (2) the central conflict that unfolds across the narrative.

Given our interest in subunits, we will naturally be asking how the scenes in a narrative relate to one another. In Genesis 12:10-20, I have divided the subunits, coded the repetition, and provided subunit titles for Genesis 12:10-13, 14-16, 17-20 (fig. 2.3).[2]

As we look at these scenes and their relation, we can look for points of tension or conflict in the story. As modern readers, *we* might feel elements of tension in reading the story: "Was it okay for Abram to leave Canaan?" and, "Is it okay for Abram to lie?" But our focus at this point should *not* be on the tension we feel as modern readers. Our focus should be instead on what the author is highlighting. What we need to look for are the elements of tension or conflict that the author is organizing the story around—this will give us a key look into what the story aims to convey.

The central tension in the plot centers on *survival*. From the start, in subunit one (Gen 12:10-13), we hear twice that the famine was so severe that it forces Abram and Sarai to migrate to Egypt. What is more, most of this subunit shows Abram scheming to preserve his own life at Sarai's expense. They have got to be desperate to be fleeing to Egypt. As readers, we leave subunit one wondering if they will survive their flight to Egypt.

---

[2]Abram is the same person who is later called *Abraham*. God changes Abram's name to Abraham in Genesis 17.

**Genesis 12**

Abram schemes on way to Egypt, preserving his life at Sarai's expense

Sarai taken to Pharaoh because of her beauty, and Abram blessed

God intervenes to save Sarai

¹⁰Now there was a <u>famine</u> in the land, and Abram went down to <u>Egypt</u> to live there for a while because the <u>famine</u> was severe. ¹¹As he was about to enter <u>Egypt</u>, he said to his wife Sarai, "I know what a <u>beautiful woman</u> you are. ¹²When the Egyptians see you, they will say, 'This is his <u>wife</u>.' Then they will kill me but will let you <u>live</u>. ¹³Say you are my sister, so that I will be treated well for your sake and my <u>life</u> will be spared because of you." /

¹⁴When Abram came to <u>Egypt</u>, the <u>Egyptians</u> saw that Sarai was a very <u>beautiful woman</u>. ¹⁵And when Pharaoh's officials saw her, they praised her to Pharaoh, and she was taken into his palace. ¹⁶He treated Abram well for her sake, and Abram acquired sheep and cattle, male and female donkeys, male and female servants, and camels. /

¹⁷But the LORD inflicted serious diseases on Pharaoh and his household because of Abram's <u>wife</u> Sarai. ¹⁸So Pharaoh summoned Abram. "What have you done to me?" he said. "Why didn't you tell me she was your <u>wife</u>? ¹⁹Why did you say, 'She is my sister,' so that I took her to be my <u>wife</u>? Now then, here is your <u>wife</u>. Take her and go!" ²⁰Then Pharaoh gave orders about Abram to his men, and they sent him on his way, with his <u>wife</u> and everything he had.

**Figure 2.3.** Text of Genesis 12:10-20

After anticipating grave danger in Egypt, Abram's scheme works, he survives, and experiences prosperity—albeit at Sarai's expense—in subunit two (Gen 12:14-16). Although this feels like a resolution, subunit two is just one step along the plot toward survival.

It turns out that the narrator cares about Sarai's survival too. Subunit three (Gen 12:17-20) brings us to the climax, where disease strikes Pharaoh, and then the conflict resolves with Abram and Sarai surviving and being reunited. Abram had endangered his wife to protect his own life, but the climax puts a spotlight on how God intervenes to strike Pharaoh and reunite Sarai with Abram.

By following the plot in light of its rise, climax, and resolution, we can see what the focal point of the passage is: the survival of *both* Abram and Sarai, as husband and wife. The repetition of terms like "wife" underscore this.[3]

*Look for the depiction of the characters, especially with God as the main character.* A major way biblical narrative conveys its message is through its characters. Physical descriptions are rare in biblical narrative, so we learn about characters through their speech and action.

Sarai does nothing active in this narrative. Abram tells her his plan, Pharaoh takes her, and God intervenes to save her. This does not mean Sarai is unimportant, but it forces us to ask what role she plays in this narrative. Abram, Pharaoh, and the narrator all describe her as Abram's wife and as beautiful. Although our modern sensibilities might object to reducing Sarai to her status as wife of Abram and her beauty, these elements are what make Sarai central to this story. We will return to this.

Abram is a more developed character here. Actively, Abram goes down to Egypt and tells Sarai his plan in the first subunit.

---

[3]Often we want the author to evaluate Abram's horrific treatment of his wife on this occasion, but the plot development shows the main interest is in God's ability to preserve Sarai and Abram's lives. This does not mean that the Bible approves of Abram's treatment of his wife; it just shows that moral evaluations are not always the aim of the narrators.

In the second and third subunits, Abram's role is passive—he receives wealth from Pharaoh, is rebuked by Pharaoh, and sent away by Pharaoh. Abram's only words are his scheming plan to preserve his own life by putting his wife in danger. With Abram's characterization revolving largely around securing and experiencing his own survival, it is clear that Abram has nothing to do with his wife's deliverance.

Pharaoh is another major character here. Pharaoh is of interest to the extent he relates to Sarai and Abram. Initially, in subunit two, Pharaoh takes Sarai into the palace as a wife, and he blesses Abraham. In subunit three, Pharaoh experiences God's wrath so that he will release Sarai and send them off.

Although Sarai, Abram, and Pharaoh have their roles to play, God is the most significant character in this passage. Did you notice who shows up right at the climax and resolution? "But the LORD inflicted serious diseases on Pharaoh and his household because of Abram's wife Sarai" (Gen 12:17). In this one verse, everyone receives mention. But it is the LORD who saves the day. He strikes mighty Pharaoh, saves barren Sarai, and reunites her with Abram. If we miss out on how God is acting, then we miss the boat on what the passage is showing about how God acts within history in his unfolding story.

If we look at the role of all these characters, they find their orbit within a plot to preserve life, not merely to preserve Abram's life but to also preserve Sarai and restore her to Abram as his wife. As we will see in step three, this is important because the Abraham narrative in Genesis 12–25 revolves around Abram having offspring through Sarai. Even if Abram survived through his scheming, the larger story could not continue without Sarai remaining Abram's wife. God made sure that happened.

Thus, when reading narrative, be alert to the plot and to the role of characters, especially, within the story. This will help us detect what is most central in the story. In steps three through six, we will return to this story to unpack it more.

*Poetry.* Poetry is the second most common genre in the Bible after narrative. Poetry breaks through the linear parts of life to help us see God, ourselves, and the world in new and memorable ways. Books like Job, Psalms, Proverbs, Ecclesiastes, and Song of Solomon are often called "Poetical Books." All of the prophets, except for Ezekiel and Jonah, use poetry far more than any other genre too. There are also poems sprinkled across the narrative books of the Old and New Testaments, such as Hannah's prayer in 1 Samuel 2:1-10 or Mary's song in Luke 1:46-55.

These poems differ in their functions. Psalms address God through hymns, thanksgiving, or lament. Proverbs offer maxims of wisdom. Song of Solomon expresses love. The prophets are mouthpieces for God, indicting God's people, warning of judgment, and promising salvation. Yet, they all use poetry to accomplish their purposes.

There are two features of poetry to home in on.

*Follow parallelism from one line to the next.* In English, we think of rhythm and rhyme as the key to a poem's flow: *Jack and Jill went up the hill . . .*

In biblical poetry, rhythm and rhyme don't animate a poem's flow. Instead, what you find is parallelism—how thoughts in one line correspond with the thoughts in the next as a way of developing and extending meaning. Consider Psalm 2: "Why do the nations rage and the peoples plot in vain?" (Ps 2:1 ESV). It is easy to see how "nations" parallels "peoples," and "rage" parallels "plot in vain" in these two lines. Although the two lines are parallel, this does not mean they are identical; it is a mistake to treat them as if they are each saying the *same* thing. Usually the second line will *advance* and build on the thought of the first. In Psalm 2:1, the second line fleshes out what the nations' raging involves—the raging manifests itself in their "plots." So, the flow moves from the outrage of the nations to the particular out-working of this by plotting.

Parallelism goes beyond just the relationship between two lines. Just like an icicle that grows one drip at a time, so the flow of poetic parallelism builds and builds and builds until the poem concludes. Check out how Psalm 2:2-3 builds on Psalm 2:1.

> The kings of the earth set themselves,
>> and the rulers take counsel together,
>> against the LORD and against his Anointed, saying,
> "Let us burst their bonds apart
>> and cast away their cords from us." (Ps 2:2-3 ESV)

At the end of verse 1, we did not know what the peoples are plotting. Now, in Psalm 2:2-3, we get further specifics. The "kings" and "rulers" represent the "nations" and "peoples" of Psalm 2:1 by advancing the thought to the leaders of the nations. We also learn why their plotting is in vain—they are plotting a rebellion against the LORD and his anointed one.

So, the key question for us to always be asking in poetry is "How does each line develop the thought unfolding across the entire poem?" Paying attention to parallelism between lines and to line after line will enable you to grasp the flow of thought and see where the message of the poem is heading.

*Let the imagery help you see what the passage is getting at.* Figurative language is part of everyday life. Even if you don't live near the coast, you could say, "Coast is clear." Even if there is no fire, you might say, "That was lit!" Even if you aren't talking about a sport, you can say "This is a game changer." In figurative language, you speak about one thing in terms of another. Usually figurative language expresses an abstract concept by using concrete imagery.

For some reason, folks get uptight when we start talking about figurative language in the Bible. The worry is that if we take something in the Bible to be "nonliteral" then we are denying the *literal* truth of the Bible. However, figurative language is a great way to convey something true. After all, even if Jesus isn't actually a door, a gate, or a lamb, we learn something true about him through these figurative images.

When we come across figurative language in the Bible, we can just ask a simple question: "What is this image trying to help me see?" Let's look at an example of this by seeing how the imagery unfolds across the parallel lines of Isaiah 1:5-6.

Why will you still be struck down?
　　Why will you continue to rebel?
The whole head is sick,
　　and the whole heart faint.
From the sole of the foot even to the head,
　　there is no soundness in it,
but bruises and sores
　　and raw wounds;

they are not pressed out or bound up
>    or softened with oil. (Is 1:5-6 ESV)

These verses describe Israel, the chosen nation of God. As you can readily see, God is trying to help his people see that not all is okay with them, his chosen nation.

The first line poses a question that implies that the audience has already been struck down, yet this striking is continuing. The second line poses a question that clarifies why they continue to be struck down—they continue to rebel. So, we are invited to see a people "struck down" and persisting as "rebels" in the opening two lines.

The imagery shifts in the second half of Isaiah 1:5. From the second half of Isaiah 1:5 through to the end of Isaiah 1:6, the imagery is that of sickness and injury. The body parts call to mind the entirety of the body: head and heart, foot and head. The range of injury types is vast too: sick, faint, no soundness, bruises, sores, and raw wounds. The end of Isaiah 1:6 brings a layer of irony to this imagery—nothing is being done to treat these wounds!

So, if we ask what Isaiah 1:5-6 wants us to see, we see rebels that are struck down yet continuing to rebel. Their wounds are immense, yet nothing is being done to treat them. The imagery invites Israel into a new way of seeing themselves, and hopefully shocks them into seeing how absurd it is to keep rebelling against God. They are in a mess because they are doing nothing to treat their wounds—they need to return to God so his judgment of them will stop. Through this imagery, they (and we) powerfully see the need to tend their (and our) wounds by turning back to God.

*Law.* Law is another popular genre on God's playlist. Don't jump too quickly to thinking about legislation, as "law" in the Old Testament often refers to instructions that help Israel cultivate wisdom and live faithfully. Laws are given to instruct Israel in how to live in God's presence and in God's world as God's holy people. The most prominent collections of laws occur in Exodus (Ex 20–23; 34), Leviticus, and Deuteronomy. Two insights into how law works will help us to more effectively read this genre.

*Figure out whether it is a general law or a case law.* A general law is a straightforward law that isn't tied to a particular scenario. The scholarly term for this is *apodictic* law. Here are some examples:

- You shall not murder (Ex 20:13)
- You shall not steal (Ex 20:15)
- You shall love the LORD your God with all your heart and with all your soul and with all your might (Deut 6:5)

These general laws are commanding Israel in how they are to live through "shoulds" and "should nots."

Case laws differ from general laws in that they give instructions related to particular scenarios that are often already messy and not ideal. Often, case laws have an "if . . . , then [consequence]" or a "when . . . , then [consequence]" construction. The scholarly term for this is *casuistic law.* For example, "If a man steals an ox or a sheep, and kills it or sells it, he shall repay five oxen for an ox, and four sheep for a sheep" (Ex 22:1). This obviously relates to the general law quoted above ("You shall not steal"), but now it is applied to a specific case that spells out how the violation should be handled within Israel. By no means do the

case laws exhaustively cover every scenario, but they help cultivate a sort of wisdom as to how such cases are to be handled.

*Identify what sphere(s) of life a law is addressing.* There is no
one right way to classify the laws we find in the Bible. For instance,
some might distinguish between laws that are *vertical*—like the
first four of the Ten Commandments that speak to how Israel is
to relate with God—and the *horizontal*—like commandments
five through ten, that spell out how to relate to others. There is a
significant limitation to this division though: obeying or disobeying any of the commandments has the potential to honor or
dishonor God and to benefit or harm one's neighbor.

Some people, especially those indebted to John Calvin, classify the laws according to moral, ceremonial, and judicial law.
For instance, "You shall not kill" is clearly a moral law. The
instructions about sacrificial offerings or clean and unclean are
ceremonial. And judicial or civil law refers to how a court might
handle a particular violation, like the man who steals an ox or
sheep. The usefulness of this classification is that it helps new
covenant believers distinguish the moral laws that endure today
and the civil (pertaining to the governance of society within
national Israel) and ceremonial (pertaining to rituals unique to
old covenant sacrifice and cleansing) laws that were peculiar to
ancient Israel.

The challenge with all of these divisions is that there can be
overlap of categories in one single law. For instance, in the Sabbath commandment, is this vertical or horizontal, ritual or
moral? All of the above. Additionally, types of laws are not
grouped within the Bible separately from one another; instead,
laws related to all of these categories are intermingled. A quick

look at Leviticus 19 shows commands pertaining to love for neighbor and immigrants (moral), to prohibitions of idol making and guidance on sacrificial offerings (vertical, ceremonial), and to dealing with sexual violation within the context of betrothal (civil). What we clearly see is that God's laws address all aspects of life within Israel.

Although we will have more to say about "law" in steps three and four, identifying whether a law is general or case law and detecting what aspect(s) of life a law is addressing takes us a long way in identifying the flow of a law. Most importantly, we must recognize that these instructions are meant to help Israel live well as a nation in the presence of a holy God.

*Letters.* The New Testament is full of letters written from an apostle to one of the earliest churches—they account for twenty-two (including Revelation) out of the twenty-seven books in the New Testament. These letters teach churches about gospel truths and direct them to live as Christ's people. Here are two bits of advice on finding the flow of a passage in a letter.

*Identify the part of the letter you are reading.* Knowing the basic layout of ancient letters is crucial at this point. Here is the typical arrangement:

- author(s) identified
- recipients identified amidst greeting
- thanksgiving
- body
- closing

Think back to our example from Ephesians 2:1-10 earlier in this step. This is part of the body.

*Find the main idea through arrowing.* In the New Testament letters, Paul and the other authors use long sentences. In Greek, Ephesians 1:3-14 is all just one sentence. Our English translations have broken some of these into a few sentences, but it is still hard for our minds to track what goes with what. To help, I draw arrows to keep track of what a clause or phrase is referring to.

To begin, it helps to distinguish between a clause and a phrase. A *clause* is a complete unit of speech that has a subject, verb, and often an object. So "I love God" is a clause because it has a subject ("I") and a verb ("love"). "The love of God" is not a clause because it has no verb; it is a *phrase*, as it does not contain a verb.

Differentiating between an independent clause and a dependent clause can be useful too. An *independent* clause can occur on its own as a complete sentence ("I love God"). A *dependent* clause cannot stand on its own, as it depends on an independent clause: I love God [independent clause] because he loved me first [dependent clause]. In "arrowing," you are trying to figure out the main, independent clause that everything is depending on.

Here is what I suggest. As you read a sentence, put brackets around each clause, as I have done in figure 2.4. Then draw an arrow between these clauses or phrases to show what belongs with what. Have a look at the example from Ephesians 2:1-2.

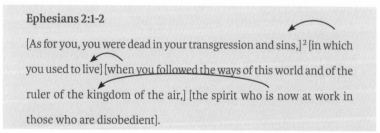

**Ephesians 2:1-2**

[As for you, you were dead in your transgression and sins,]² [in which you used to live] [when you followed the ways of this world and of the ruler of the kingdom of the air,] [the spirit who is now at work in those who are disobedient].

**Figure 2.4.** Text of Ephesians 2:1-2

The flow of thought in this verse all hinges on this one, independent clause: "You were dead in your transgressions and sins." All the arrows ultimately point back in its direction. We will call this the MC (main clause)—it is a sentence that can exist on its own (an independent clause). Just like spokes on a wheel, all of the rest of Ephesians 2:1-2 leads back to this MC. "As for you" shifts attention to the "you" in the MC. All of Ephesians 2:2 unpacks the "transgressions and sins" from the MC—a previous way of life characterized by following the ways of the world and Satan, who continues his work among the disobedient. Paul's focus, then, is to spell out the audience's status as once dead in their sins.

As you continue arrowing across each subunit, clarity with regards to the flow of the passage will increase. Arrowing keeps us active as we read, and it helps us find the flow of passages in these letters with their flowing didactic sentences. If you aren't into marking your Bible, you can actively trace these movements by pointing with your finger. Another option is to copy the text from an online Bible into a blank word-processing document and print it out.

## CONCLUSION

In my office hangs a painting of the prophet Isaiah by Irving Amen. It is my prized possession. I have developed a weird habit. I will stand just inches away from it and stare at the minute brush, pencil, and pen strokes. When I'm up that close, the different strokes, colors, and textures seem completely unrelated. However, as soon as I step back, I can see how these all *flow* together to present a stunning sketch of Isaiah.

Similarly, sometimes when we read the Bible it can feel like we are seeing lots of unrelated words, phrases, and sentences. Step two recommends two tricks of the trade that will help us find the flow of a passage: subunits and genres.

So, how does finding subunits and attending to genre coordinate as you read the passage? No matter what genre you are dealing with, let identifying subunits lead the way in identifying the flow. Then with those subunits in place, cycle back through the passage with an eye toward its genre and let this enrich your sense of the flow within those subunits.

Ultimately what we are after in this step is a close reading of the passage to better grasp what the original author intended to communicate through the passage as a whole. Step three will build on this.

If we follow these tips for finding the flow of your passage, we are adding essential fuel to the furnace that the Holy Spirit can set ablaze to help us hear God's voice as we sit at his feet.

## DISCUSSION QUESTIONS

1. Describe your experience of looking for subunits in Ephesians 2:1-10. What was helpful? What was difficult? Did you discover anything new?

2. Practice identifying subunits using Genesis 22:1-19. What does the flow of this passage help you to understand about its meaning?

3. How might adopting the practice of seeing God as the main character affect the way you read biblical narratives? What might you do differently from what you have done before?

4. Practice tracing parallelism and noting imagery in Isaiah 35. What does this practice add to your understanding of the text?

5. Explain in your own words why genre is important for reading and interpreting a biblical text.

*Step 3A*

# Context

Historical

"CONTEXT IS KING," SAY BIBLE TEACHERS. As we consider step three, I hope you will come to see why. I anticipate that you will return to this material in step three over and over again as a source of information while you read the Bible. There are two types of context to keep in mind: historical and book context.

Since a great deal of information needs to be provided about both the historical and book context, I've decided to divide these into separate chapters: step 3A and step 3B. Don't let the amount of information here fool you. Over time, as you gain familiarity with both types of context, practicing step 3A and 3B will seem less like two steps and more like one step that involves two vantage points.

## THE IMPORTANCE OF HISTORICAL CONTEXT

Early in my journey with Jesus, I was preaching from John 4—the story where Jesus offers living water to a Samaritan woman. Early in the sermon I honed in on this sentence: "It was about the sixth hour" (Jn 4:6). "Why is it important to know Jesus arrived at 6 a.m.?" I asked rhetorically. "Because it shows Jesus had to flee into the dangers of night to get away from persecution in Jerusalem."

I camped out on this 6 a.m. arrival for a while, drawing out how dangerous it would have been to travel at night on unlit roadways. My focus was on how bad the persecution must have been in Jerusalem for him to flee at night. Here's the problem. I was wrong. "The sixth hour" is not 6 a.m.; it is noon at the time of Jesus. There was no flight by night.

*Backgrounds* illuminate the historical, social, and cultural context of a passage. The ancient Near East (ANE) is the background of the Old Testament. Greco-Roman and Jewish backgrounds bring light on the New Testament.

In the same sermon, I emphasized how Jesus offers her living water because the Samaritan woman had been trying to quench her thirst through men, for Jesus says, "You have had five husbands, and the man you now have is not your husband" (Jn 4:18). Here's the problem: I was wrong to sexualize this statement. At that time, a divorce could happen during an engagement or when a man sees that marrying someone else would enhance his social standing. Marriages could also end due to untimely deaths of husbands. The fact she had five husbands says more about the hardship she faced than about her promiscuity.

What is more, the fact she was living with a man not her husband is not automatically an indictment. She could have been prohibited by law from marrying this man due to differences in social status. After all, if she was a promiscuous and socially shameful woman, why would all of these men have married her and why would the entire village believe her when she tells them about Jesus?[1]

If I had been more accurate about the historical context, I would have understood that Jesus was not offering spiritual water as a way of replacing her quest to find refreshment through sex. No, Jesus is revealing his divine knowledge of the life of hardship she had experienced.

So, if we want to better understand God's Word, we need to take historical context seriously. God acts and speaks in real times and places, so it should be no surprise that God's Word comes to us historically situated.

For some of us, reading about history is like a dreaded chore. What's the point of learning about the historical times of the Bible? Here are a few thoughts that might help.

Reading the Bible is like a crosscultural experience. We wouldn't think twice about the need for a new missionary in Syria to learn the culture, history, and geography of Syria. Similarly, when it comes to reading and understanding the Bible, some crosscultural and historical knowledge goes a long way. If God's Word was written in the contexts of the ancient Near East and the Greco-Roman world, then surely understanding these contexts will enrich our reading of God's Word.

Another way to see the value of studying history is through the idea of ancestry. Ancestry.com is a $5 billion business because so many of us want to know more about our family

---

[1]For more on this, check out Caryn A. Reeder's *The Samaritan Woman's Story: Reconsidering John 4 After #ChurchToo* (Downers Grove, IL: IVP Academic, 2022).

history and, in the process, ourselves. Similarly, our ancestry links back to Adam, and, through faith in the second Adam (Jesus), all Christians become part of Abraham's offspring too (Gal 3:29). This means that the family history of the Bible is our own family history. Learning about the contexts within which our family history unfolds will help us know our own story better, particularly how our God relates to and what he expects from his chosen family.

When attempting to better grasp God's Word as conveyed in its historical context, here are three key questions to learn to ask:

- *When* is this taking place?
- *Where* is this taking place?
- *How* does the passage fit within the culture of the time?

I'll answer each of these questions for each testament by presenting a timeline (when), a geographical overview (where), and common cultural dynamics (how).

Although I highlight select elements in the backgrounds of each testament, I would recommend that you invest in a study Bible, particularly one that is more historical or archaeological in nature. My favorite is by John Walton and Craig Keener, *The Cultural Backgrounds Study Bible* (NIV or NRSV). It provides comments on each page of the Bible, along with maps, timelines, charts, and more.

## OLD TESTAMENT

In the movie *Midnight in Paris*, a wannabe writer named Gil is wandering around the streets of Paris. When midnight strikes, he is transported back to the 1920s but doesn't know it. We are then treated to some hilarious scenes where Gil is meeting famous artists, writers, and musicians from the past, and he doesn't know how to make sense of anything. When he meets the famous author F. Scott Fitzgerald, Zelda Fitzgerald, his wife, says to Gil, "You have a glazed look in your eye, stunned, stupefied, anesthetized."

Have you ever felt glassy-eyed, stupefied, or even anesthetized when you drop into an Old Testament passage? The Old Testament speaks of thousands of years past. If you'd feel out of place in your grandparents' generation, imagine how odd life thousands of years ago would seem.

**When *is this taking place?*** A first step in getting oriented within the historical context of the Old Testament is to simply ask, "When is this taking place?" To answer this question, begin by consulting a general Old Testament timeline (see fig. 3A.1).

Let me offer a few comments along the eight phases in the Old Testament timeline. We will fill in the significance of these phases within God's redemptive story in step four.

*1. Primeval History.* The timeline begins in Genesis 1–11 with Primeval History. *Primeval* means the "earliest of times." These chapters include stories about God creating, humans sinning, and God judging sin and showing grace in the stories of Adam and Eve, Noah, and Babel. It is very difficult to assign dates to these events. If we are reading in this section, we should be asking how these accounts set the stage for the rest of the timeline.

*2. Patriarchs.* Next we move on to the Patriarchs in Genesis 12–50. *Patriarch* is a Latin term meaning "founding father."

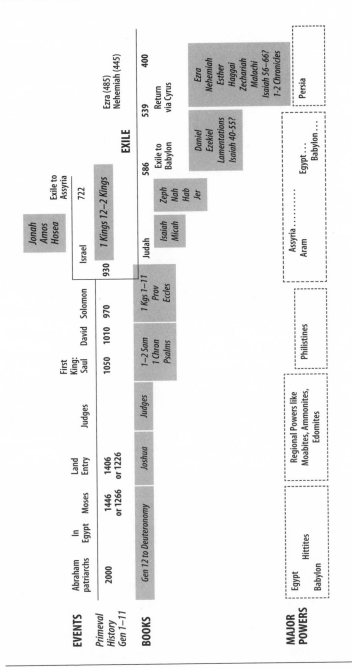

**Figure 3A.1.** Old Testament timeline

Abraham, Isaac, Jacob, and Jacob's twelve sons belong to this group. This period of history recounts God's involvement with Abraham's family to multiply and preserve it. The events here are set during the start of the second millennium BC when Egypt is the superpower, and Israel is not yet a nation. Abraham and his family own no property in Canaan except for a burial site. They are nomads, slowly growing in number and wealth and moving to find pastureland and water for their herds. By the end of Genesis, the entire family ends up in Egypt. As you read about the era of the Patriarchs, be mindful of how the storyline zooms in on one family (Abraham's) and how God multiplies and preserves this marginal family in Canaan, Mesopotamia, and Egypt.

3. *Egypt, Sinai, and the Wilderness.* The next phase in the timeline recounts Israel's deliverance from Egypt and their meeting with God at Mount Sinai. After hundreds of years in Egypt, Israel is populous yet enslaved. God raises up Moses to lead his people out of Egypt. Some date the exodus to 1446 BC and others to around 1266 BC. After God delivers Israel out of Egypt through Moses (Ex 1–15), they travel down the Arabian Peninsula to Mount Sinai where they camp and meet with God for over a year. From Exodus 19 to Numbers 10, God is preparing Abraham's numerous family to live as a holy nation by providing them with instructions—Torah ("instruction" or "law"). If you are reading Exodus, Leviticus, and the first part of Numbers, be alert to God's power to save Israel from Egypt and how God's law at Sinai aims to guide Israel to live as a nation. From Sinai, Israel travels across the wilderness toward Canaan. Israel doubts that God can dispossess the Canaanites and give them the land, so

God punishes Israel and makes them wander in the wilderness for forty years (Num 11–36). At the end of forty years, Israel camps at the edge of the Promised Land and Moses preaches to Israel to prepare them to live as God's chosen people when they possess the land (Deuteronomy). When reading Numbers and Deuteronomy, consider how God is using the forty-year delay and Moses' sermons to prepare Israel to be a holy nation once they enter the land.

4. *Conquest and Judges.* The fourth phase in the Old Testament timeline involves Israel's possession of and early years in the Promised Land. Under Joshua, Israel enters Canaan and God provides several victories. The conquest of the land is limited to a few small regions in the east, southeast, and northeast. The majority of the land—especially along the coast—remained unconquered. During this time, God would raise up regional judges to deliver his people from oppression. Religiously, the tribes of Israel look a lot like the Canaanites, with their recurring cycles of idolatry. When reading Joshua, Judges, and Ruth, consider Israel's possession of the land, their repeated failure to obey God's instructions from Sinai, and God's graciousness to raise up judges as deliverers.

5. *United Monarchy.* After living in the land for a few hundred years under judges, Israel requests a king. Samuel identifies Saul as Israel's first king in 1050 BC, but King Saul does not obey God and thus will have no dynasty (1 Sam 8–15). When David becomes king in 1010 BC, he makes Jerusalem the political and religious capital of Israel. Though David wants to build God a temple there, God says no and declares that he will build a house for David. David's dynasty would be on the throne

forever. David's son Solomon takes over as king in 970 BC, builds the temple, and extends Israel's borders. This is the golden age of Israel. Many psalms connect with David, and Wisdom books with Solomon. You can read about these eras when Israel lived as one nation under one king (united monarchy) in 1–2 Samuel, 1 Kings 1–11, and 1 Chronicles 10 to 2 Chronicles 9. So, when reading these books, be alert to the political shift to kingship and to God's commitment to David and his descendants. Although the reigns of David and Solomon display God's blessing through Davidic kingship, David and Solomon's failings make clear that Israel's idyllic golden age would not last.

6. *Divided Monarchy.* In 930 BC a major rupture takes place. As punishment for Solomon's idolatry, God divides the nation in two: Judah and Israel. Judah is the nation to the south, with Jerusalem as its capital and with Davidic kings ruling. Israel is the nation to the north, consisting of ten tribes, having Tirzah and then Samaria as its capital and having kings from nine different dynasties. Two major sins plague Israel: oppression of the poor and idolatry. So God raises up prophets like Elijah, Amos, and Hosea to confront Israel and warn that God's judgment was coming through the expanding empire of Assyria. In 722 BC, the death knell sounds for Israel; Assyria destroys Samaria, takes Israel into exile, and settles foreigners in the land. Judah does not escape God's judgment either, with prophets like Isaiah, Micah, Jeremiah, and Ezekiel warning Judah that the next Mesopotamian superpower—Babylon—is coming. In 586 BC, Babylon levels Jerusalem and its temple, slaughters the Davidic king's children, and takes many into

exile. The Divided Monarchy is a dark, dark era religiously and politically. Books set during this era include 1 Kings 11 to 2 Kings 25, 2 Chronicles 10–36, Isaiah 1–39, most of Jeremiah, most of Ezekiel, Hosea, Amos, Jonah, Micah, Nahum, Habakkuk, and Zephaniah. If you are reading passages in these books, be alert to whether or not Israel or Judah is in view, to what sins God is addressing, and to the threat of Assyria or Babylon.

7. *Exile.* Exile refers to a time when many from Israel (722 BC) and then the upper class of Judah (586 BC) are forced to migrate and live in Mesopotamia and Egypt due to invasions by Assyria and Babylon. All of the symbols that show they are God's people are gone: the temple is destroyed; Davidic kingship is absent; the people are uprooted from the land. With Abraham's offspring now either in foreign lands or living amidst the rubble of Canaan, exile becomes a time for grief, self-examination, doubt, and new vistas of hope. Lamentations, along with some psalms, gives voice to the trauma of terror and loss when Jerusalem fell. Isaiah 40–55 offers hope to exiles. Daniel models faithful living in Babylon. The latter parts of Jeremiah and Ezekiel are also set during exile, in Egypt and Babylon. During this phase of the Old Testament timeline, ask how exile became a time to lament, to live faithfully, and to cling to hope.

8. *Post-Exile.* In 539 BC, King Cyrus of Persia takes over all of the territory controlled by Babylon. He issues a decree that those wishing to return to the Promised Land may do so. A small fraction returns to Jerusalem to rebuild the temple. Later Ezra returns (458 BC) to institute religious reform through obeying

Torah. Nehemiah then (445 BC) leads efforts to rebuild the walls of Jerusalem. During this time of social and religious renewal, God continues to provide prophets (Haggai, Zechariah, Malachi) to energize the people and to confront sin. If you are reading Ezra, Nehemiah, Haggai, Zechariah, or Malachi, pay attention to a focus on renewal back in the land of promise amidst trials. If you are reading Esther, this gives you a window into Jewish life during the Persian era for those who did not return to Jerusalem.

In summary, there are eight phases in the timeline of the Old Testament. Consider revisiting the paragraphs above when you branch into new parts of the Old Testament in your Bible reading. Detecting where a passage is on the timeline begins by asking the question: *When* is this taking place?

**Figure 3A.2.** Eight phases in the Old Testament timeline

| Era | Books of Bible | Noteworthy Events |
|---|---|---|
| 1. *Primeval History* Difficult to date | Genesis 1–11 | Creation, Fall, Flood, Babel |
| 2. *Patriarchs* 2100–1600 BC | Genesis 12–50 | Abraham, Isaac, Jacob, and 12 sons |
| 3. *Egypt, Sinai, and Wilderness* 1446–1406 BC or 1266–1226 BC | Exodus Leviticus Numbers Deuteronomy | Deliverance from Egypt Law given at Sinai Wandering in Sinai desert for 40 years due to sin |
| 4. *Conquest and Judges* 1406 BC or 1226 BC—1010 BC | Joshua Judges Ruth 1 Samuel 1–7 | Partial conquest under Joshua Judges deliver from oppression |
| 5. *United Monarchy* 1010 BC–930 BC | 1 Samuel 8–31 2 Samuel 1 Kings 1–11 1 Chronicles 10–29 2 Chronicles 1–10 Some psalms Some wisdom books | Kingship starts with Saul, David, and Solomon Jerusalem capital, temple built |

| Era | Books of Bible | Noteworthy Events |
|---|---|---|
| 6. *Divided Monarchy* 930–586 BC | 1 Kings 11–22 2 Kings 2 Chronicles 10–36 Isaiah 1–39 Jeremiah Ezekiel Hosea Amos Jonah Micah Nahum Habakkuk Zephaniah Some psalms Some wisdom books | Two nations: Israel and Judah Two empires: Assyria and Babylon Judgment of idolatry and oppression through exile |
| 7. *Exile* Sixth-century BC | Lamentations Isaiah 40–55 Daniel Jeremiah Ezekiel Some psalms | Life after Jerusalem's ruin and in foreign lands |
| 8. *Post-Exile* 539 BC–onward | Ezra Nehemiah Esther Haggai Zechariah Malachi | Cyrus decrees a return Rebuilding of temple and city Commitment to the law |

**Where *is this taking place?*** "The land is the playing board of the Bible," says an archaeologist friend of mine. Imagine trying to play chess without the board. You'd be lost. To understand the moves in the Bible, you need to see and understand the board. So, a good habit to develop when reading in the Bible is to ask, "Where is this taking place?" Over time, you will develop greater and greater familiarity with the geography of Israel and the ancient world if you regularly consult relevant maps.

Let's consider two maps—a map of Israel and a map of the ancient Near East.

*The land of Israel.* On the map of Israel (figure 3A.3), notice the four regions from west to east.

- The *coastal plain* is the richest of areas in Israel. Ports along the coast enabled trading vessels from across the Mediterranean Sea to import and export goods. The coastal plain's flat contour made it a major travel route. The Philistines lived in this cosmopolitan and international region for much of the Old Testament.

- The *central hill country* is where Israel, and later Israel and Judah, lived. The hill country is naturally insulated from enemies. It has decent soil on its slopes for terraced farming of grapes and olive trees, while its valleys work well for grain. The frequently mentioned cities of Jerusalem, Bethel, and Samaria were tucked into this region.

- The *Jordan Valley* surrounds the Jordan River, drops below the sea level, and is quite barren. It stretches along the Jordan River from the Sea of Galilee to the Dead Sea. David spent a great deal of time hiding from Saul in this region.

- The *Transjordanian Plateau* is the territory to the east of the Jordan River. Three tribes received it as an inheritance, but it was usually occupied by Ammon, Moab, and Edom.

If you move from north to south, several items are noteworthy. The northern region around the Sea of Galilee is a fertile area with ample rainfall. Baal worship became prominent in this region, as Israel adopted this god of rain from Phoenicia. In the far south, there is the Negev. The Negev is a desert region, and the Patriarchs spent a fair amount of time there.

**Figure 3A.3.** Regions of ancient Israel

Finally, on the map you will see the territory of Judah (930–586 BC) in the south and Israel (930–722 BC) to the north during the divided monarchy. In Judah, observe how Jerusalem is the capital. In Israel, note how the two sites Jeroboam set up to worship golden calves are in the far north (Dan) and the south (Bethel). Nuzzled in between is Samaria, Israel's capital from the time of King Omri until its fall.

*The ancient Near East.* Our next map provides a view of where Israel fits within the surrounding ancient Near East (fig. 3A.4). God knew what he was doing when he chose the land of Canaan. Notice how Canaan sits at the crossroads between the major powers of the time.

The two most powerful regions were Egypt and Mesopotamia. To Israel's southwest, you will notice Egypt. The Nile enabled life to flourish along its banks in Egypt. Similarly, to Israel's northeast, you will see the region of Mesopotamia. The Tigris and Euphrates provided the water necessary to turn Mesopotamia into the breadbasket of the ancient world. The northern part of Mesopotamia was Assyria and the southern part, near the Persian Gulf, was Babylon.

Naturally, the great civilizations in Egypt and Mesopotamia would trade with one another and smaller peoples would want to trade with these powers as well. The main routes for travel from Egypt to Mesopotamia would be up the coastal plain of Israel, then through Galilee, and then through Damascus to the Tigris and Euphrates. One could branch further east into Persia from Mesopotamia. Merchants from Arabia would travel through Israel as well to reach these areas. Ships from the Mediterranean would use ports along

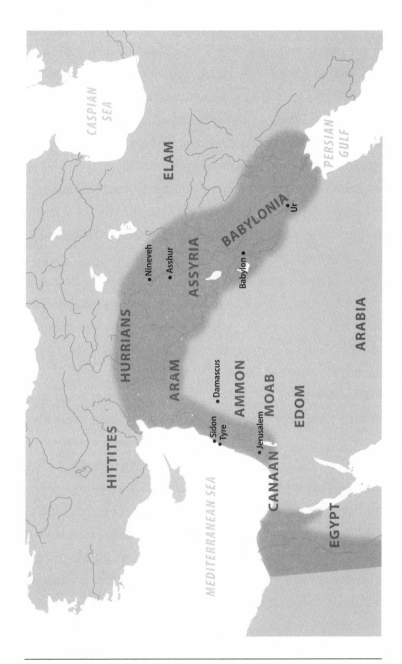

**Figure 3A.4.** Ancient Near East

the coast of Israel to bring goods for trade throughout this region.

Israel was prime real estate due to its central location between empires and along a seacoast. As a result, there are few phases in Israel's history when the dominant empire of the time did not control or try to control Israel, whether it be Egypt, Assyria, or Babylon. When these major empires were waning in power within the region, the smaller nations surrounding Israel would seize the opportunity to fight, whether it be Aram to the north or Ammon, Moab, and Edom to the east and southeast.

God knew what he was doing by putting Israel at the crossroads of the known world. Israel would need to trust God as they were surrounded by greater nations. More significantly, Israel's central location could enable it to be a light to the surrounding nations.

**How *does this fit within the culture of the time*?** When missionaries receive training, they prepare for culture shock and develop skills for learning a new culture. We need the same skills when reading the Bible. God gave us an Old Testament that was originally written to people living in a culture vastly different from Western society. In many respects, those from Africa, the Middle East, and Asia might be able to comprehend more easily what I may find puzzling. Developing cultural competence is a long journey. As a starter, here are three prominent features in ancient Israelite culture: family and land, honor and shame, and mountains.

*Family and land.* If I were to ask someone in Wheaton, Illinois, "What is our society built around?" they would probably say things like, "democracy," "fair treatment of every individual," "education," or "political parties." In ancient Israel, the answer would likely be "family and land." The two belong together.

God owns the Promised Land, and Israel is sojourning in his land (Lev 25:23). Within this setup, God allows each tribe and, within that, each family line to possess a portion of land. Family land would pass from one generation to the next through first-born sons as an inheritance. Recognizing this helps make sense of property allotment in Joshua, why Naomi returns to Bethlehem in the book of Ruth, laws related to property, and the shame of kings for confiscating land from the people.

The land is not simply a place to live. It is central to daily life. Great-grandparents, grandparents, parents, and children, along with aunts, uncles, and cousins, would contribute to the essential tasks of cultivating, harvesting, and processing what sprung from the land. Some plowed, planted, irrigated, and harvested grains. Others pruned and picked grapes and olives. Others winnowed and pressed. Still others turned these gifts from God that sprung from the land into food that would grace the table.

There is, however, a major challenge for families in the land—no rivers for irrigation. They need rain. If they obeyed God, he would provide rain. If they disobeyed, he would withhold rain (Deut 11:10-17). The land is the avenue through which God would extend his blessing or curse to his people, and rain or drought is often an indicator of whether or not Israel would experience blessing.

This dependence on rain creates a grave temptation to turn to local storm and fertility gods. As a result of such idolatry, God sends a drought during the time of Elijah to show that he, not Baal, is the true God of the storm (see 1 Kings 17). God sends prophets like Hosea to confront such sin and reveal God's broken heart over their turning away from him to other gods.

If you come from more individualistic and nonagrarian cultures, it may take time to be alert to the family-land dynamic. Once your eyes are opened to it, a great deal in the Old Testament will make more sense.

*Honor and shame.* In the ancient Near East, honor and shame are significant drivers of behaviors and interactions. In such societies, honor comes to those who uphold what the group values and shame comes on those who do not. In comparison, an innocence and guilt dynamic is more prevalent in Western society. In the West, we are driven by an internal, individual moral compass. If we violate our conscience, we feel guilty; if we don't, we feel innocent.

Consider adultery. Someone in the West who resists a temptation to commit adultery is likely driven by an internal sense that adultery is wrong. In an honor-shame culture, the major motivator is different—one would resist adultery to maintain one's honor and their family's honor within the community.

Consider Adam and Eve. Before they ate the forbidden fruit, "they were both naked, and they felt no shame" (Gen 2:25). But as soon as they eat, they realize they are naked and cover themselves (Gen 3:7). They even try to hide from God (Gen 3:8). It is shame that drives Adam and Eve to shield themselves from one another and God.

Here is another example from Genesis. When Abraham's wife Sarah dies, he wants to buy a cave to bury her in Machpelah (a town in Canaan). So he meets with the elders of the town at the gate. The owner of the land, Ephron, begins by indicating that he would give Abraham the land for free. If we were Abraham, we'd probably say, "Okay! I'll take the deal. Thanks for your charity." But Abraham knows Ephron's offer is the honorable gesture in such circumstances, so Abraham insists on paying for the land (also the honorable behavior). So Ephron says, "My lord, listen to me: a piece of land worth four hundred shekels of silver, what is that between you and me?" (Gen 23:15). Do you see what just happened? Ephron just names his price without demanding this from a widower. Abraham readily detects this and pays him 400 shekels. Ephron and Abraham make it through this deal with their honor intact—Ephron shows sensitivity to Abraham's being a widower and Abraham pays for the property.

As a final illustration, consider a law in Deuteronomy 25. It is laced with honor and shame. If a brother marries and then dies without a son, another brother is to marry the widow and the firstborn son will "carry on the name of the dead brother so that his name will not be blotted out from Israel" (Deut 25:6). But check out what happens if a brother refuses to marry his dead brother's wife. He is to be paraded before the elders, and then the wife of the dead man will "take off one of his sandals, spit in his face and say, 'This is what is done to the man who will not build up his brother's family line.' That man's line shall be known in Israel as The Family of the Unsandaled" (Deut 25:9-10). Honor is at stake in one's decision. If the brother of the deceased does not do the honorable thing, his family will receive a shameful nickname: "The Family of the Unsandaled." These are just a few examples to encourage us to be alert to honor and shame in the Old Testament.

*Mountains.* Mountains are the third cultural element in the Old Testament to consider. At first glance, we might wonder what makes mountains a cultural element. Consider how differently Americans view mountains in comparison to the ancient Israelites. When I want to hike a mountain in Colorado, I use my All-Trails app to find out about the conditions, the degree of difficulty, and hiker ratings. But the AllTrails app is missing what would be of most interest to an ancient Israelite: What god resides on that mountain? Mountains were thought to be the meeting place between heaven and earth, between the gods and humans.

Two mountains dominate the storyline of the Old Testament: Mount Sinai and Mount Zion. Mount Sinai is where God meets with Moses to establish a covenant of law keeping. Mount Zion is in Jerusalem, where the temple is built and where God's presence fills it. Since Zion is the meeting place between God and Israel, it is central to life in Israel. They stream there for worship at festivals. The psalmists sing of its beauty because God lived there (Ps 46; 48). The prophets envision a time when God's presence at Zion would be so great that all the world would stream there (Is 2:2-4).

More negatively, mountains are also a temptation. Since Judah and Israel lived in the hill country, there were hilltops around every corner. This is why we read so regularly of false worship taking place at "the high places."

By being aware of the significance of mountains, we can more readily interpret Psalm 121:1, a passage we considered in step two: "I lift up my eyes to the mountains, where does my help come from?" Why does the psalmist lift his eyes to the mountains? Looking to the mountains is symbolic of looking to the place where God steps into our world to meet with us. Unlike other local gods, the helper the psalmist looks to is the maker of heaven and earth (Ps 121:2).

Thus, by way of summary, being alert to when events are taking place, where they take place (geography), and how a passage fits within the culture of the time will enable us to understand the Old Testament better. Now that we have more perspective on the timeline, geography, and culture in the Old Testament, it is time to turn to the New Testament.

## NEW TESTAMENT

**When** *is this taking place*? In comparison with the thousands of years of Old Testament history, the timeline of the New Testament is much shorter—100 years.

There are five significant phases in the New Testament storyline.

*1. Jesus.* Jesus' birth, ministry, crucifixion, resurrection, and ascension span from approximately 5 BC–AD 30.[2] This was a time when the Roman Empire controlled Palestine (more below), with Augustus and Tiberius as Caesars. The local ruler at the time of Jesus' birth was Herod the Great, who was known for his tremendous building projects, including the temple in

---

[2]The calendar was set for the Western Church in the 500s AD, when a monk named Dionysius undertook the task of creating a calendar that pivoted around AD, *anno domini* (the year of the Lord). Unfortunately, Dionysius misplaced Christ's birth. Herod the Great died sometime between 4 BC and 1 BC, so Jesus' birth is before Herod's death, between 7 BC and 5 BC.

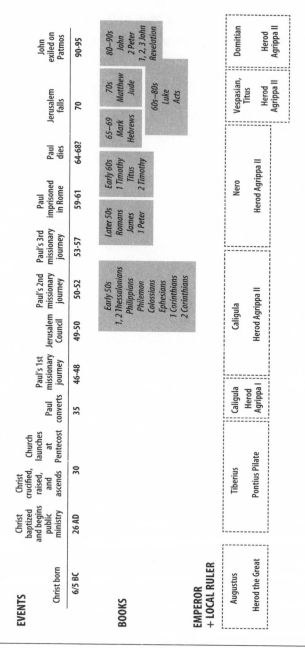

**Figure 3A.5.** New Testament timeline

Jerusalem. During Jesus' ministry, Herod Antipas was ruler in Galilee while Pontius Pilate ruled in Jerusalem. The Gospels—Matthew, Mark, Luke, and John—recount the good news of Jesus' life, death, and resurrection during this era, but the Gospels themselves were not written until the 60s–90s AD, though there were certainly collections of stories about Jesus circulating early on. Before Jesus ascended to heaven, he told the disciples to wait in Jerusalem. He says, "You will receive power when the Holy Spirit comes on you; and you will be my witnesses in Jerusalem, and in all Judea and Samaria, and to the ends of the earth" (Acts 1:8). The threefold movement from Jerusalem to Judea and Samaria and to the ends of the earth gives structure to phases two, three, and four in our New Testament timeline.

2. *Pentecost in Jerusalem.* At Pentecost, in the year of Jesus' ascension (AD 30), the Holy Spirit came like a rushing wind on the disciples in Jerusalem (Acts 2). The disciples spoke in other languages, testifying about Jesus as the risen Messiah. Then Peter preached a sermon that results in over 3,000 people believing in Jesus. This marks the launch of the church.

3. *Spreading to Judea and Samaria.* As the church grew in Jerusalem, so did persecution. As a result, many disciples scattered beyond Jerusalem. Leaders such as Philip and Peter brought the good news of Jesus to towns throughout the land of Israel (called Judea at the time). As God's Word spread, the inclusion of non-Jews, known as Gentiles, is a focus in Acts. An Ethiopian eunuch is baptized by Philip (Acts 8), and a vision propels Peter to enter the home of a Gentile military leader in Caesarea named Cornelius who was waiting for a word from God. Peter then declares the message of Christ, and the Holy Spirit comes on all gathered at

Cornelius's home (Acts 10). God was making clear that his church would include both Jew and Gentile, but by the end of Acts 12 the gospel had not been preached beyond the borders of Judea and Samaria.

*4. Paul's witness to the ends of the earth.* In Acts 13, approximately fifteen years after Christ's ascension, Paul is set apart to declare the good news of Jesus beyond Israel's borders. He goes on three missionary journeys that encompassed Asia Minor (modern-day Turkey), the island of Cyprus, and the region of Greece. Persecution follows Paul throughout his journeys, and by the end of Acts, Paul winds up in Italy, on house arrest in Rome as he awaits a hearing from Caesar. During these travels, including seasons of imprisonment in Ephesus and Rome, he writes many letters to the churches he had previously established or to their daughter churches.

*5. Christianity amid continuing persecution.* From the death of Jesus through Paul's imprisonment, persecution was part of the church's experience. This theme continues beyond the timeline of Acts (AD 60). In AD 64, a fire broke out in Rome, which Emperor Nero blamed on Christians, resulting in their persecution. Nero's concern with Jews extends to Palestine, when the Jews attempt to revolt against Roman rule in AD 66. Nero then sends his general Vespasian to siege Jerusalem. By AD 70 Jerusalem is ravaged, and Vespasian is the new emperor. The destruction of Jerusalem had a significant impact on how the growing Jewish sect of Christianity would view their faith. Finally, Emperor Domitian (AD 81–96) is likely responsible for having the author of Revelation banished to the island of Patmos. It is unclear if Domitian supported the systematic persecution of

Christians, but during his reign Christians in various places faced persecution. The book of Revelation is written to encourage believers to persevere during these times of grave trial.

Thus, there are five phases in the New Testament timeline. As you read different books in the New Testament, develop the habit of asking what phase a given book belongs to.

**Figure 3A.6.** Five phases in the New Testament timeline

| Era | Books of Bible | Noteworthy Events |
|---|---|---|
| 1. *Jesus* 5 BC–AD 30 | Matthew, Mark, Luke, John | Birth, life, death, and resurrection of Jesus |
| 2. *Pentecost in Jerusalem* AD 30 | Acts 2 | Holy Spirit descends; 3,000 converts |
| 3. *Spreading to Judea and Samaria* 30–40s AD | Acts 3–12 | Peter and Philip bring the gospel to Judea and Samaria (including Gentiles living there) |
| 4. *Paul's Witness to the Ends of the Earth* 40s–60s AD | Acts 13–28 Most of the NT letters | Paul and companions spread the gospel to Gentile nations |
| 5. *Christianity amid Continuing Persecution* 60s–90s AD | Revelation | Jerusalem falls; increased persecution of Christians |

**Where *is this taking place*?** Jesus' life and ministry unfold in the land of promise. As you see in figure 3A.7, two regions are most prominent during Jesus' time on earth: Galilee and Jerusalem.

The vast majority of his life and upbringing is in the region of *Galilee* in the northern part of Israel. Jesus grows up in Nazareth, a tiny town below the poverty line. Jesus then picks Capernaum as his ministry headquarters. Capernaum sits on the northwestern shore of the Sea of Galilee. This is where a number of his disciples, including Simon Peter, are from. With Capernaum as a hub, Jesus can easily travel to towns throughout the region of Galilee.

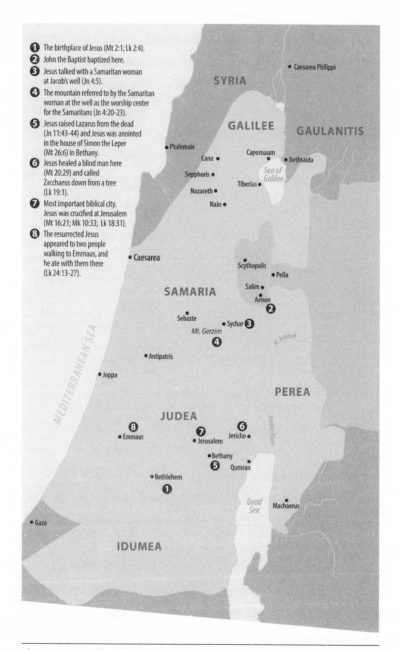

**Figure 3A.7.** Jesus' life and ministry

The second region for Jesus' life and ministry is *Jerusalem and Judea*. Notice how Samaria—a region and people that Jews typically avoid—stands between Galilee and Jerusalem. This creates a regional difference between those of Jerusalem and Judea and those of Galilee; Galileans even have an accent different from those living in Jerusalem. What is more, Jesus would branch into Samaria to show God's desire to include outcasts in his kingdom. In Jerusalem, Herod had rebuilt the temple, so Jesus joins with many Jews of the time to travel there for festivals. Ultimately, it is in Jerusalem where Jesus would be crucified and rise again.

Turning now to figure 3A.8, we see Paul's three missionary journeys. On the first journey, Paul goes to the island of Cyprus and then moves on to several cities in the eastern part of Asia Minor (modern Turkey). On the second journey, Paul takes an inland route to cities throughout Asia Minor, crosses over to Macedonia and Achaia (modern Greece), and then has a lengthy stay in Ephesus before returning to Jerusalem. Paul's third journey involves revisiting many of the cities from his earlier trips. As he faces continued persecution, Paul's appeal to speak before Caesar results in a journey to Rome.

**How *does this fit within the culture of the time*?** Some of what we spoke about regarding the cultural dynamics in the Old Testament remain relevant as we read the New Testament. Due to exile and Roman occupation, the land-family dynamic from the Old Testament is less prominent in New Testament times. Honor and shame, however, appear all over the place. Joseph didn't want to shame Mary by publicly divorcing her. The story of the prodigal son revolves around a son shaming himself and his father, yet the father shames himself by welcoming back his

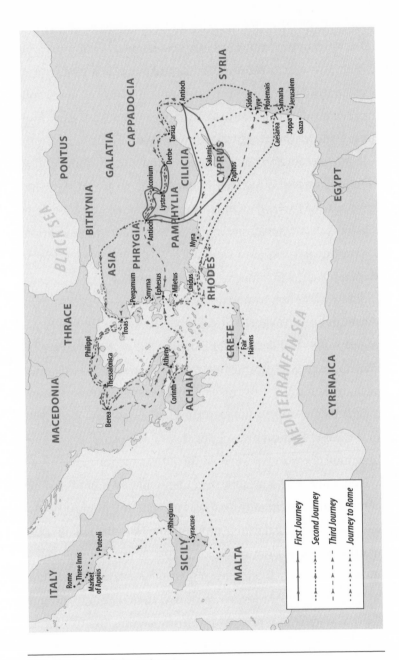

**Figure 3A.8.** Paul's missionary journeys

son and honors him with a party. Mountains remain in view too in New Testament times, as one sees in Jesus' Sermon on the Mount and the conversation between Jesus and the Samaritan woman in John 4.

There are two significant cultural dynamics during the New Testament era that we should know about.

*Life under Roman rule.* Roman rule touches all of life for first-century Jews and Christians. Rome calls a census, so Mary and Joseph travel to Bethlehem. Rome requires taxes, so some Jews become tax collectors. Rome demands stability in its provinces, so Roman governors and military battalions ensure this is the case.

Just think of how significant Rome is in the story of Jesus. The decree of Caesar Augustus to take a census marks the beginning of Jesus' life. The decree of a local Roman governor—Pontius Pilate—permits Jesus' crucifixion. The crime Jesus is condemned of is treason against Rome, as only Caesar is king. So Jesus is mocked with a robe, a thorny crown, and a sign that read "King of the Jews." He becomes a bloody spectacle on a Roman cross to remind the world of the dangers of insurrection.

Rome too casts a shadow over Paul's ministry, as he and his companions continually face arrests and potential imprisonments for the gospel Paul is proclaiming—there is a king other than Caesar: Jesus. Rome's extensive road systems do ease Paul's travels across the empire. Rome's use of Greek as the common language enables Paul to readily speak with those he came across. Paul even appeals twice to his Roman citizenship, to prevent false imprisonment and also as a way of booking a ticket to Rome. There is no getting around the fact that his declaration that Jesus is Lord is not only good news but also politically dangerous during a time when Caesar alone was called lord (Acts 17:7).

*First-century Judaism.* Amid Roman rule, Judaism is the heartbeat for Jews during the first century in Israel. Dietary habits, ritual cleansing, and Sabbath-keeping infiltrate daily life. Central locations, such as the temple in Jerusalem and synagogues in other cities, are gathering points for Jews. Synagogues play an important role in preserving Jewish culture, as they served as schools, worship centers, and places to gather for civic matters. Jesus visits synagogues across Galilee as he went from town to town, and Paul's pattern is to begin his ministries in new cities by speaking with Jews in their synagogues.

Jewish life at the time of Jesus had three major groups: Pharisees, Sadducees, and the Essenes. The largest group is the *Pharisees*. The Pharisees are laypeople who devote themselves to teaching and obeying the law as scholars and teachers. They identify 613 laws in Torah and take seriously the need to obey them. For instance, the Torah teaches to keep the Sabbath. To give guidance on practicing the Sabbath, the Pharisees draw on other verses to specify that one should stay close to home and not leave city limits. In addition to these laws, Pharisees believe in the afterlife and angelic beings. Jesus regularly interacts with the Pharisees who are concerned with his violations of Sabbath rules and his associations with the unclean. Paul describes himself as a Pharisee.

The *Sadducees* are another group we encounter in the Gospels. Also devoted to Torah, they differ from the Pharisees in several ways. They come from the upper class, only obey what is specifically spelled out in the Torah rather than traditions, and do not believe in resurrection or angelic beings.

The *Essenes* are a group of zealous Jews that are separatists. They hold that Jews who associate with Rome are tainted. They live in communities in isolated places in the Jordan Valley, such as Masada and Qumran. They believe that the end of the world is at hand, but the Messiah would not come until they are living in purity.

In addition to these three groups, priests and scribes receive mention throughout the Gospels. During the time of Jesus, priests have a responsibility for serving in the great temple built by Herod in Jerusalem. The High Priest would wield tremendous power both religiously and politically, with Annas and Caiaphas receiving mention in the Gospels. Scribes come from every group of Jews and were spread throughout Israel. Some were priests, others Pharisees, and yet others worked in trade. Their chief task was interpreting and teaching Torah. So, when we ask *how* the New Testament fits within the culture of its time, we should be alert to Roman rule and the strands of Judaism that were part of everyday life.

## SUMMARY

Learning to read the Bible in view of its historical contexts is like moving from black-and-white to high-def TV. For both testaments, we offered a timeline, maps, and a few cultural insights. These spring from three key questions we should ask whenever reading a passage:

- *When* is this taking place?
- *Where* is this taking place?
- *How* does the passage fit within the culture of the time?

In addition to learning to ask these questions, we will find benefit from having a study Bible or commentary at hand to gain historical insights into specific passages.

We can now turn to the second type of context to be mindful of: book context.

*Step 3B*

# Context

Book

IF YOU ARE A BIBLE PROFESSOR, random questions come your way at family gatherings. On one such occasion, my sister-in-law says, "So, Andy. We're studying 1 Samuel in my women's Bible study. This week we were studying 1 Samuel 14, and we had no clue how it might apply to us. What are your thoughts?"

Wow. Straight from talking about kids and dirty diapers to my thoughts on 1 Samuel 14. I knew the passage talked about King Saul's son Jonathan bravely fighting foes, Saul vowing that whoever tastes food that day will die, Jonathan eating honey, and Israel intervening to prevent King Saul from killing Jonathan. But what in the world are my "thoughts" on how to apply the passage?!

My brain raced. Then a moment of clarity came, and I said, "With any passage we need to ask: *Why* has this passage been included *here* in the book?" I went on to talk about how in the surrounding chapters there are stories about King Saul failing to obey God and declarations that Saul's dynasty would not continue (1 Sam 13; 15). So, we need to think about how 1 Samuel 14 is contributing to the picture of Saul as a terrible king.

In 1 Samuel 14, Jonathan is braver than Saul. Saul makes rash vows, and, if it weren't for Israel, he would have killed his own son like pagans do. These stories illuminate how Saul isn't a great king.

But the failure of Saul in 1 Samuel 13–15 does more than show us that Saul is bad. Saul's rejection prepares us to hope for a king who is much different from Saul—a king after God's own heart (1 Sam 13:14). We meet this king in 1 Samuel 16, David. Then in 1 Samuel 17 we see David bravely trusting God when he faces Goliath. The application is really for us to see our need for a king far different from Saul.

I am drawing on the *book* context, also called *literary* context, to help clarify what the author is actually trying to accomplish through 1 Samuel 14. We must learn to ask, "*Why* has this passage been included *here* in the book?"

Here are two tips when trying to read a passage within its context in a book.

## TIP 1: READ THE PASSAGES SURROUNDING YOUR PASSAGE

A simple step is to look at the passages right before and right after the passage you are studying. How does your passage advance from what comes before? How does the passage following build on your passage?

*Ephesians 2:1-10.* Let's return to a passage we analyzed in step two, Ephesians 2:1-10. In step two, we arrived at the following summary statement of the passage after identifying its subunits: *We were dead in our sinful course of life, but God graciously made us alive in Christ to give us a new way in life, one of doing good works.*

So, the question now is: *Why* is Ephesians 2:1-10 included *here* in the book? Looking at the preceding passage (Eph 1:15-23) unveils a mind-blowing connection. Paul is praying that the Ephesians will know the power of God that is at work among believers. He describes God's power as the very power that *"raised Christ from the dead* and *seated* him at his right hand *in the heavenly realms"* (Eph 1:20). Amazingly, what happened to Christ according to Ephesians 1:20 is said to have happened to us in Ephesians 2:1-10. I've italicized the similarities between both passages: "God, who is rich in mercy, made us alive with Christ even when we were *dead . . .* and *raised* us up with Christ and *seated* us with him *in the heavenly realms"* (Eph 2:5-7). Do you see it?! What God did for Christ God has also done for us! When Christ rose from the dead, we too rose from the dead. When Christ took his seat in heaven, we too sat down with him in the heavenly realms. Our journey from death to life in Ephesians 2:1-10 is anchored in the power of Christ's journey from death to life (Eph 1:15-23).

When we look at the following passage (Eph 2:11-21), a new layer of significance emerges too. Paul opens Ephesians 2:11 with "therefore." As a pastor of mine used to say, "You need to ask what the 'therefore' is there for." The "therefore" tells us that Ephesians 2:11-21 is an implication or consequence of Ephesians 2:1-10. He spells out how Christ makes it possible for both Jew and Gentile to be united as the joint dwelling place of God.

But what does Ephesians 2:1-10 have to do with this vision of reconciliation in Ephesians 2:11-21? If the story of all Christians—Jew and Gentile—is sharing in Christ's death, resurrection, and ascension (Eph 2:1-10), then this has implications on earth—Jew and Gentile are together a united dwelling place for God's Spirit. By simply reading the passages before and after, we can more readily decipher what a passage aims to communicate.

*Genesis 12:10-20.* Another passage we examined in step two was Genesis 12:10-20. Most are baffled about what to do with the story of Abram and Sarai heading to Egypt and Sarai becoming Pharaoh's wife until God intervenes. In step two, applying the steps of narrative to this passage (plot, characterization, etc.) brought us a long way toward seeing the emphasis on God intervening to deliver Sarai to reunite her with Abram. We need, however, Genesis 12:1-9 to truly unlock the importance of God delivering Sarai.

At the start of Genesis 12, God calls Abram to leave his life in Mesopotamia and go to the land God shows him. In Genesis 12:2, God promises "I will make you into a great nation, and I will bless you" (Gen 12:2). There is tremendous irony in this promise. Just before this, we are told that "Sarai was childless because she was not able to conceive" (Gen 11:30). Yet, God calls a seventy-five-year-old man (Gen 12:4) to leave everything and promises to turn him into a great nation. The obvious tension here pertains to how an elderly, barren couple could become a great nation.

If we read Genesis 12:10-20 through the lens of the promise of offspring, then the reason why God saves Sarai becomes clearer: God's plan to turn Abram into a great nation will come through Abram *and* Sarai as a pair, so God intervenes to deliver her from the powerful Pharaoh. Nothing thwarts God's ability to keep his promises.

Not only do the surrounding passages bring the promise of offspring into view in Genesis 12:10-20, but the promise of land seems to be important too. Just prior to the trip to Egypt, God leads Abram to the land of promise and says, "To your offspring I will give this land" (Gen 12:7). The promise occurs while Abram and Sarai are sojourning throughout Canaan (Gen 12:5-9).

Just after the trip to Egypt in Genesis 12:10-20, we read of Abram and Sarai's return to Canaan: "So Abram went up from Egypt to the Negev" (Gen 13:1). Genesis 13 goes on to recount Abram's division from Lot in order to specify the dimensions of Canaan that God is giving to Abram.

With a focus on land prior to and after Genesis 12:10-20, we come to see what God's deliverance of Sarai and Abram has to do with land. God shows his power to restore his people to the land of promise, even in the face of grave danger in Egypt. This story could very well be a prelude to how God will save Israel from the land of Egypt in order to bring them to the land flowing with milk and honey.

Through these examples, I hope you can see the value of tip one. Reading the passages before and after your passage will bring into focus what we might otherwise miss.

## TIP 2: GROW IN GRASPING THE ENTIRE BOOK

When I was in seminary, one of my professors told us about a minister who would not preach from a passage until he had read that book of the Bible fifty times. Don't worry. I'm not going to recommend that you read Genesis fifty times.

Here are a few realistic steps toward grasping the big picture of a given book of the Bible.

1. When doing a Bible study, study in a passage-by-passage sequence from the beginning to the end of a book. Don't hop from passages in one book to another. A sequential approach through a book of the Bible will help us more naturally sense how a passage fits within the book's unfolding message.

2. Nearly every study Bible will begin each book of the Bible with an outline. As you read the book, track where you are in light of the outline of the book.

3. The Bible Project has incredible videos called "Book Overviews" that sketch the overall shape of each book and its major themes. These are free and available on their website (bibleproject.com) or YouTube. I highly recommended that you watch one whenever you start a new book.

4. If the opportunity arises, read through the entire book, tracing major shifts in thought and keeping track of where themes in your passage pop up elsewhere in the book.

*Genesis.* Let's return to Genesis 12:10-20. How does the entire structure of the book illuminate the contribution of Genesis 12:10-20?

To begin, notice how a popular study Bible divides Genesis into two major sections:

   I. Primeval History (Gen 1:1–11:26)

  II. Patriarchal History (Gen 11:27–50:26)

*Primeval* refers to the earliest stages of the world. This is an appropriate title for Genesis 1–11 because these chapters begin with God's design in creation (Gen 1–2). Next, they recount how sin against God results in disharmony between God, humanity, and the world (Gen 3–11). So, Genesis 11 leaves us with a global vantage point on humanity—we are bent toward rejecting God and are thus scattered across the entire world under the curse of death.

*Patriarchal* refers to the founding fathers of Israel: Abraham, Isaac, Jacob, and Jacob's twelve sons. This is an appropriate title for Genesis 11:27–50:26 because they tell the stories of this family.

There is an obvious shift, then, from world history in Genesis 1:1–11:26 to the history of one particular family line (Abraham's) in Genesis 11:27–50:26. This structure shows us that God's plans and promises to Abram must be understood in light of the depiction of the entire world in Genesis 1–11. With the entire world in rebellion against God and experiencing life far from the ideal in Eden, God sets into motion a plan to redeem the entire world through one particular family. So God says to Abram, "All the peoples of the earth will be blessed through you" (Gen 12:3).

What light does this shine on our reading of Genesis 12:10-20? As we saw above, yes, God is showing his unbreakable commitment to turn Abram and Sarai into a great nation (offspring) and to give them the land of promise. The larger structure of Genesis helps us see that God's intervention in Egypt is part of his even wider purpose to bring blessing to the entire world through the family of Abram.

In addition to observing the general, two-part structure of Genesis, we also benefit from observing the more immediate section of Genesis to which our passage belongs. The *toledoth* ("These are the generations . . .") headings open the major sections of the book, and ours opens in Genesis 11:27 with "Now these are the descendants of Terah" (NRSV). As Abram is a descendant of Terah, this is an apt title for stories largely relating to Abram, one of Terah's sons. This section stretches from Genesis 11:27–25:18.

If we scan across Genesis 11:27–25:18, we can see a recurring interest in God's commitment to provide offspring through Abram *and* Sarai.

- Genesis 12: God promises Abram, aged seventy-five, offspring.

- Genesis 15: Abram fears because he is childless, and God promises him descendants as numerous as the stars.

- Genesis 16: Abram and Sarai utilize Hagar as a surrogate who bears Ishmael.

- Genesis 17: Abraham, aged ninety-nine, laughs when God tells him that the promised child will come through Sarah.

- Genesis 18: Sarah laughs when God announces that she will give birth one year later.

- Genesis 20: God again delivers Sarah from the house of a king to ensure there is no doubt as to who is the father of Sarah's child.

- Genesis 21: Sarah, at age ninety, gives birth to a son whom they name Isaac, meaning "he laughs."

- Genesis 22: God saves Isaac from slaughter and provides an alternative sacrifice.

It is apparent, then, that the narrative arc of Genesis 11:27–25:18 revolves around whether God will fulfill his promise to provide offspring to Abraham and Sarah. One strategy in this section focuses on the obstacle of age. Abram and Sarai receive the promise at ages seventy-five and sixty-five, and we see God wait until they are one hundred and ninety to fulfill the promise. It is unmistakable that God is responsible for the miraculous creation of Israel.

A second strategy focuses on the obstacle of foreign kings. God delivers Sarah from Pharaoh and later from Abimelech. When seen in this light, we can see how Genesis 12:10-20 figures into the section's aim of showing God's ability to fulfill his promise of offspring in the face of severe obstacles, including the threat of kings.

A general awareness of the section within Genesis that Genesis 12:10-20 is part of helps us highlight its contribution to the book: God's faithfulness to make good on his promise to create a nation out of Abram and Sarai, even in the most precarious of circumstances.

## CONCLUSION

Context—both historical and book—is king indeed. Here is a set of questions we identified in relationship to historical context (step 3A):

- *When* is this taking place?
- *Where* is this taking place?
- *How* does the passage fit within the culture of the time?

The key question to ask as it relates to book (literary) context (step 3B) is:

- *Why* has this passage been included *here* in the book?

Our tips for answering this question are to read the passages before and after the passage you are studying and to factor in the organization of the particular book of the Bible in view.

The focus of steps two and three has been on recovering what God inspired a human author to communicate to an original audience through a given book. The technical word for this is exegesis—attempting to draw out what a passage would have meant to an original author. In step four, we will add an additional dimension to interpretation—God's intention for each book of the Bible to be part of a sixty-six book, two-testament Bible that bears witness to Jesus.

## DISCUSSION QUESTIONS

1. In what ways is it familiar or new for you to think about reading a passage within its historical and book contexts?

2. Can you think of a time when learning the historical context of a biblical passage helped you to understand its meaning in a new way? If so, what was it?

3. Can you think of a Bible verse or passage that is often quoted out of context (e.g., Jer 29:11; Phil 4:13)? If so, watch a book overview of that book from bibleproject.com and read the passages before and after your passage. Does this change your understanding of the verse or passage? If so, in what ways?

4. It can feel like a lot of work to study historical and literary contexts when you simply want to read the Bible. What are the benefits of putting in this work? Why does it matter to your study of Scripture?

*Step 4*

# Whole Bible

ONE DAY, MY KINDERGARTENER, BETHANY, enthusiastically announces, "I painted a rock today in art class!"

I play along: "That is so cool! What did you paint on it?"

She tells me: "It is purple with pink dots!"

I was a bit puzzled about the excitement.

Then my third grader, Anna, chimes in with the bigger picture: "For the end of the year, the art teacher is going to make a rock garden out of all of our rocks." Anna painted hers with a sparkly purple backdrop, a black middle, and yellow dots—like a galaxy. The art teacher will then spray the rocks with a protective glaze and arrange them strategically into a beautiful garden around a tree at their school.

This might be a stretch, but the Bible is like this rock garden. Each book of the Bible is a uniquely painted stone, with its own flowing passages and historical and book contexts. Yet, God is like an art teacher. He adds a shimmering protective glaze to preserve each book and brings all sixty-six together into a single book, the Bible. The individual rocks still retain their beauty, but the garden resulting from their preservation and combination is far more stunning.

There is one limitation to this analogy. A rock garden gives the impression of a random assortment of beauty. The Bible, however, has a very strategic arrangement, much like tiles in a mosaic or the threads of a tapestry. And God was inspiring the author to write a book that would become part of a beautiful whole.

Up to this point, in steps two and three, our focus has been on individual stones, tiles, or threads. We've been trying to understand what a passage means in its original context. But here's the thing—God had something bigger in mind all along. He wasn't simply creating sixty-six standalone books. No, God had plans to arrange these books together to create a Jesus-shaped portrait. This brings us to "Step 4: Whole Bible." In this step, we ask how a passage points to Jesus and plays a role in the Bible's redemptive story.

## POINTING TO JESUS

Ever wonder how a compass works? Magnetics. The little needle in a compass is magnetic, and so is the magnetic north pole. Since the needle is attracted toward the magnetism of the North Pole, it will always spin to align its point toward the north. Jesus is the magnetic north of the Bible. All Bible passages find their bearings through alignment with him.

In Luke 24, two disciples walk sadly toward Emmaus. The resurrected Jesus joins them, but they have no clue who he is. They share about how their hopes have been dashed—the one they hoped to be the Messiah is dead and his body is now missing. Then Jesus says to them, "'How foolish are you, and how slow to believe all that the prophets have spoken! Did not the Messiah have to suffer these things and then enter his glory?'

And beginning with Moses and all the prophets, he explained to them what was said in all the Scriptures concerning himself" (Lk 24:25-27). Do you see what Jesus did? He shows how all of those needles in the Bible point to the magnetic north revealed in Jesus. As the disciples listen, their hearts burn.

Throughout the New Testament, the apostles draw on the Old Testament over and over again. Matthew's genealogy tells us that we need to know Jesus in view of Abraham, David, and exile. There are nearly 300 explicit quotations of the Old Testament in the New. If we add in allusions and echoes, there are well over one thousand references to the Old Testament throughout the New Testament. Jesus' birth (Is 7:14; Mt 1:21), ministry (Is 61:1-3; Lk 4:18-19), and death (Ps 22; Is 53) are all part of God's plan from the Old Testament. For this reason, the gospel of Jesus is said to be "according to the Scriptures" (1 Cor 15:3-4).

Some think that only select passages in the Old Testament point to Jesus, but I think it is always worth pondering how each passage relates to Jesus. There is danger in this because readers can force all sorts of unlikely and unnatural connections between the Old Testament and Jesus. When we read the Old Testament in view of Jesus, we need to be sure to do so in a way that aligns with the initial meaning of the Old Testament text. The advice below aims to help you relate the entire Bible to Jesus in a way that honors and builds on what God inspired the original human authors to communicate to their audiences.

I want to begin step four, then, by offering the most straightforward way to seeing how a passage points to Jesus—looking for parallels. We will then consider how Jesus fits into the Bible's redemptive story.

## PARALLELS

The most basic question we can ask is this: What does this passage say about God, and how is this reflected in Jesus? If God has always existed as one God in three persons (Father, Son, and Holy Spirit), then what we learn about God anywhere in the Bible reveals something about Jesus' character.

If God knew from before the foundation of the world that Jesus' first and second comings would be the climax of history, then what we read anywhere in the Bible will be preparing for the moment that gives sense to all that came before and all that will come after.

A wonderful starting point, then, is to simply ponder what your passage reveals about God and how this relates to what we see in Jesus. Let's look at how this works in Genesis 12:10-20, a passage we considered in steps two and three. This is the story where Abram and Sarai escape famine by heading to Egypt.

At first glance, there does not seem to be anything in Genesis 12:10-20 about a messiah or coming king. This does not mean it has nothing to say about Jesus—remember he is God. We need to start by asking, "What does this passage teach about God?"

As we saw in step two, God enters at the climax of the story to deliver Sarai from a power she could not overcome—Pharaoh: "But the LORD inflicted serious diseases on Pharaoh and his household because of Abram's wife Sarai" (Gen 12:17). What does this passage reveal about God? It shows how God is one who delivers from the greatest of superpowers in order to keep his promises. What is more, it shows God's concern and intervention on behalf of a mistreated and vulnerable woman.

Now, if Jesus is God, then what we learn of God in Genesis 12 is true of Jesus. How do we see Jesus acting to deliver us from an insurmountable power? At the culmination of history, Jesus steps into our world to free us from powers we cannot overcome—sin, death, and the evil one.

Also, when Jesus graced this earth, he too showed tremendous care for women who were mistreated and vulnerable. Just think of how Jesus sticks up for the woman who lathers him with oil. He dines with and delivers prostitutes, and then they often play important roles in his ministry. In this way, God's actions in Genesis 12 prepare for and bear witness to the culminating revelation of God in Jesus.

This kind of reading is called a *figural* reading—an approach that believes the divine author knew how each rock was prefiguring the garden that would become clear when Jesus came.

> *Figural reading* maintains that a later revealed figure—Jesus—brings clarity to how what came before relates to him.

Here is another example from Isaiah 1. During Isaiah's time, Judah's religiosity is off the charts. They pray, sacrifice, burn incense, celebrate festivals, and worship. They seem to check all of the boxes of what would put someone in good standing with God, right? Wrong.

God announces through Isaiah that he is not listening to their prayers. He finds no pleasure in their sacrifices. He hates their assemblies. Sure, God commends these practices to Israel at Sinai, but there is a reason why such religiosity is detestable to God at the time of Isaiah: injustice.

Your hands are full of blood!

    Wash and make yourselves clean.

    Take your evil deeds out of my sight;

      stop doing wrong.

Learn to do right; seek justice.

    Defend the oppressed.

Take up the cause of the fatherless;

      plead the case of the widow. (Is 1:15-17)

The passage offers a significant window into God's heart—God desires that those who worship him via religious practice also promote justice in the world around them. He does not want one without the other. In other words, devotion to God should include a devotion to ensuring justice for the most vulnerable in our midst.

How does what Isaiah 1 reveals about God parallel what we see in Christ? Christ displays the very same heart as we see of God in Isaiah 1. Consider, for instance, Jesus' harsh words for the Pharisees: "Woe to you, teachers of the law and Pharisees, you hypocrites! You give a tenth of your spices—mint, dill and cumin. But you have neglected the more important matters of the law—justice, mercy and faithfulness. You should have practiced the latter, without neglecting the former" (Mt 23:23). Jesus is not against sacrificial giving, but, like in Isaiah, Jesus pronounces a woe over these religious folk because they are neglecting justice and mercy for the vulnerable. In this way, Isaiah 1 prepares us for a cumulating revelation of God's character when the Son takes on flesh. Jesus desires a community that both worships God and promotes justice.

The simple movement of looking for parallels between what a passage says about God and what we see in Christ is a wonderful starting point. There are other ways of relating the Old Testament to Christ, but this is an essential first step. For those wishing to go further, I would recommend either chapter five in *Preaching Christ from the Old Testament* (Eerdmans, 1999) by Sidney Greidanus or Edmund Clowney's *The Unfolding Mystery* (P&R, 2013).

One danger with figural readings is that someone might twist a passage into saying whatever they want it to say. For instance, let's take "your hands are full of blood" from Isaiah 1:15 above. It would be twisting this text if someone said this prefigures how our hands will be full of the cleansing blood of Jesus. The reason such a reading would be suspect is that it is completely out of touch with its sense within the passage—the blood on their hands indicates guilt, not forgiveness (see Is 1:18 for cleansing).

The concern over twisting texts is legitimate. Two guardrails will keep us on a good route as we navigate our way toward Jesus.

1. *Establish parallels between the passage and Jesus that align with the central message of your passage.* This is why steps two and three are so, so very important. If our parallels to Jesus have no alignment with the original meaning of our passage, then we are driving offroad toward a ditch. In the examples above, the connection with Jesus flows naturally out of the central plot in Genesis 12:10-20 (God's intervention to fulfill his promises and care for the

vulnerable) and the rhetorical aim of the prophetic poetry
in Isaiah 1:10-17 (God's call for justice).

2.  *Make sure your claims are not at odds with what the Bible
    as a whole teaches about God and Jesus.* So, for instance in
    Genesis 12:10-20, what if someone suggests that just as
    Abram gave up his bride, Sarai, for a time to Pharaoh when
    danger came, so Jesus will give up his bride, the church,
    for a time to Satan when danger comes. There are several
    problems with this. This action by Abram is not affirmed
    or a key point in Genesis 12, so there is little basis in the
    passage for emphasizing this point. What is more, the
    whole Bible teaches us that Jesus will never abandon us
    and is a good shepherd who does not abandon his flock
    when danger comes (Jn 10:10-12).[1]

With these parameters in place, invite the Holy Spirit to open
your heart to see how the passage you have been carefully studying points to Jesus by looking for parallels.

We now turn to the second way of reading in light of Jesus:
redemptive history.

## A JESUS-CENTERED STORY

A story unfolds across the Bible that centers on Jesus. This is
called redemptive history. That there even is a story unfolding
across the Bible is remarkable. The Bible contains sixty-six
books, written by at least forty human authors across a span of
over a thousand years in three languages (Hebrew, Aramaic, and

---

[1]For those less familiar with the entire Bible, the Nicene and Apostles' Creeds present a
summary of belief about what the Bible as a whole teaches about God. By becoming
familiar with these creeds, you will have helpful parameters for assessing whether
claims made about a passage are outside of the core beliefs of Christians across the ages.

Greek) and many genres. How is it possible for all of this to weave together into one grand love story of God redeeming the world in Jesus?[2]

The answer: God. Yes, God inspired *human* authors to write their individuals books, but the *divine* author also knew how the part would fit into the whole. God is the author of all sixty-six books, and he is the central subject of all of these books. He knew from eternity how the parts would fit together around himself to make a beautiful whole.

The clearest way the story of the Bible holds together is through covenant. A covenant is a solemn commitment between two parties that includes promises and often expectations. Although humans can make covenants with one another (e.g., marriage), the divine covenants are occasions where God enters into covenant with people. These covenants are stones on a path that lead to Jesus. They are the backbone of the story of the Bible.

> *Biblical theology* is a branch of study that explores how the sixty-six books of the Bible, in all of their uniqueness, hold together to create a sense of unity.

Let's walk through each part of God's covenantal love story.

*Creation, fall, and Noah: prologue to the redemptive covenants.* The story of the Bible begins with God. This God who existed in all eternity as one God—Father, Son, and Holy Spirit—chooses to create. We are not told why God creates the

---

[2]Scholars often wrestle with whether and how the wisdom literature (Proverbs, Job, and Ecclesiastes) fits into a wider redemptive story. One option is to see wisdom in closer connection with creation than redemption. If this is the case, then we can explore how the Son, the one through whom all was created, makes himself known in such wisdom.

world, but theologians suggest that it was because God wanted
to share the love between the Father, Son, and Holy Spirit with
the world.

*Creation's ideal.* Many look to Genesis 1–2 for answers to our
scientific questions about the origins of the universe, but what
if we began to look at Genesis 1–2 as the prelude to God's story
of redemption? We would find in Genesis 1–2 God's design for
the world, how things were before everything began unraveling
due to sin.

Genesis 1–2 shows us God's ideal for the world. This ideal can
be illustrated through a triangular interconnection between
three parts: God, place, and people (see fig. 4.1). The left side of
the triangle represents God's purpose to create a habitable place
on days one through three. Though the earth was initially unin-
habitable, dark, and covered with water (Gen 1:2), God creates
light, the sky and sea, and then finally an earth full of vegetation.
God creates a habitable place.

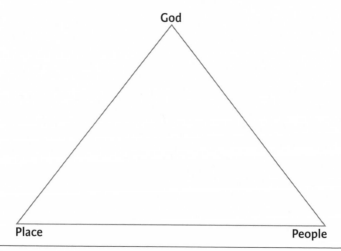

**Figure 4.1.** God's ideal in creation

On the right side, we see God's intentions on days four through six to create inhabitants, particularly people. Lights are set in the sky to shine on the earth. Animals inhabit the sky, sea, and earth. Then finally, God creates people—male and female—in his image. The bottom of the triangle reminds us of God's plan for his people to live in and be stewards of God's place, rulers of God's good world. Having completed his work, God rests, taking up residence in the world he created with his people serving as his vice-regents.

Genesis 2 emphasizes this same triangulated reality. God creates a habitable place on a smaller scale—Eden with its gardens—and sets the first human pair (Adam and Eve) within it to care for the place God created. Intimacy and peace mark all of these relationships.

Creation shows us that God's grand design is for his people to live in a place he created, where he blesses and is present with them. This ideal, however, is fragile: it depends on whether or not Adam and Eve will obey God's Word.

*Sin ruptures the ideal.* In Genesis 3, God's ideal for creation begins to rupture due to sin (see fig. 4.2). The Xs in our diagram represent fractures on all sides of the triangle. On the right, there is a rupture between God and people. Adam and Eve disobey and hide from God. They then lose access to God's special presence in the garden. Harmony between God and people is fractured. The left side shows a sad new relationship between God and place: God now curses the ground as a punishment toward Adam and Eve for their sin.

The bottom of the triangle represents how Adam and Eve's relationship to the ground will now be difficult. Thorns and thistles will hamper their cultivation of the earth. Adam and Eve are banished from the Garden of Eden. Without access to the tree of life, death will be the ultimate result of toiling to live off the cursed ground.

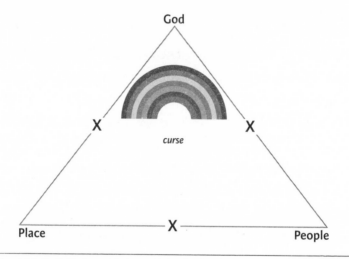

**Figure 4.2.** God's ideal unravels due to sin, but he gives hope

Yet, although God's creation ideal is fractured, hope remains. Eve's offspring would continue its battle with Satan and his minions, and ultimately her offspring would crush Satan's head (Gen 3:15). One day God's ideal for his world would be restored.

*God's covenant with Noah: Securing a fallen world.* Sin and its consequences continue in Genesis 4–11. We reach a point where "every inclination of the thoughts of the human heart was only evil all the time" (Gen 6:5). Sin leads to death, so God decrees death to all humans through a flood. Yet, in his grace, God saves one man and his family—Noah.

After the flood, God creates a covenant with Noah that reiterates his commitment to his intention for creation. The rainbow (fig. 4.2) serves as a sign in this covenant that God would never flood the earth again. This covenant creates a stable context within which the rest of the redemptive story can unfold. No matter how bad sin gets, God will not wipe out all of humanity through a flood until his redemptive mission comes to completion.

*Reading in light of creation, fall, and Noah.* Genesis 1–11 is the launching pad for the story of redemption that follows. The story of the Bible ends with a similar emphasis on the triangulated ideal that we see in creation: with God dwelling with his people in a new place, a new heaven and a new earth (see Rev 21).

No matter where we are reading in the Bible, we can ask, "What is God doing to redeem and restore his ideal for the world that has been lost due to sin—an ideal of God having a people who live obediently in a special place in his presence?"

**God's covenant with Abraham: a particular people with a universal purpose.** With sin spreading and people scattering across the world, albeit amidst the stability that comes from God's promise not to flood, God's story of redemption kicks off by narrowing in on one family: Abraham's.

As he had done before in creation, God speaks. This time he speaks to Abram (later renamed Abraham) with these words:

"Go from your country, your people and your father's household to the land I will show you."

I will make you into a great nation,
    and I will bless you;
I will make your name great,
    and you will be a blessing.
I will bless those who bless you,

> and whoever curses you I will curse;
>
> and all peoples on earth
>
> will be blessed through you. (Gen 12:1-3)

God's promises to Abraham—given here and ratified as a covenant in Genesis 15—become the lens for interpreting the rest of God's story of redemption. If God's mission is to restore the creation ideal that was lost due to sin, then the covenant with Abraham shows us that God will accomplish those purposes through Abraham's family-nation, Israel.

There are four key components in God's promises to Abraham that reflect and advance our triangular representation of God's redemptive story (see fig. 4.3). An inner triangle represents how God's covenant with Abraham shows a microscale recovery of God's creation ideals with Israel.

- *Promised Land.* Just as God created a habitable place in the beginning (left side of triangle), so God would provide a specific place for Abraham—the land of Canaan.

- *People.* Just as God created humanity as a whole as his people (right side), so God will create a great nation out of a barren couple, Abraham and Sarah. This nation will be called Israel.

- *Presence.* Just as God dwelt with Adam and Eve in Eden, so God will be uniquely present with Abraham's family-nation, blessing them and making their name great.

- *Plan to Reach the Nations.* All peoples of the earth will be blessed through Abraham's family, so God's plan for the particular people (Abe's family) is for a universal purpose. For this reason, in figure 4.3 there are channels left open at the corners of the inner triangle to show God's plans to bless the world through Israel.

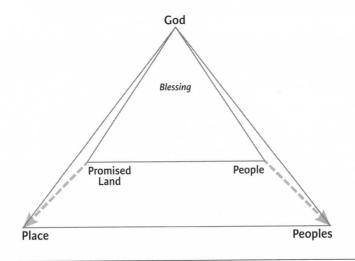

**Figure 4.3.** Covenant with Abraham: global redemption through one people

Just as God's ideal in creation was to create a habitable place within which an obedient people would enjoy God's blessing and presence, so God's promises to Abraham are a manifestation of this at a microlevel. The triangulated ideal will be seen in God's being uniquely present with a specific people (Israel) in a specific place (Promised Land) to bless the world through Israel.

*Reading in light of the Abrahamic covenant.* The Abrahamic covenant invites us to read the Bible with attention to the place of Israel in God's plans of redemption. Some might wonder: *Does it matter that Jesus was a Jew who carried out his mission in the Promised Land?* The Abrahamic covenant gives us the answer. Throughout the course of redemptive history, we need to be alert to the unfolding fulfillment of God's promises to bless and redeem the world through a chosen people (Israel) that are to uniquely experience God's blessing in a particular place (Canaan). Jesus came as a Jew to the land of promise to bring blessing to the world.

## GOING DEEPER: Promises of Abraham Today

No matter whether one is reading Joshua or John, the covenant with Abraham invites us to read through the lens of God's promises to restore his ideal in creation through being uniquely present with a particular people (Israel) in the Promised Land. For new covenant believers (see below), there are a few challenges with how to interpret promises to Abraham regarding nationhood and land today.

Yes, Jesus is the "offspring of Abraham" that blesses all nations (Gal 3:8, 14). Yes, the church is now part of the offspring of Abraham through faith in Christ (Gal 3:7, 29). So, yes, we can read of God's faithfulness to Israel throughout the Bible as a window into God's commitment to bless the church through Christ and into God's faithfulness to the family we are now part of. Yes, we can see the Promised Land as pointing to a greater fulfillment in the new heaven and new earth.

But what does this mean for the future of Israel as a national and ethnic nation? What does this mean for the land of Canaan that God promised Israel? Some say that we should look for a literal fulfillment of the nation and land promises when Christ comes again. In this view, Christ will rule over the nation of Israel in the Promised Land during a millennial reign. If this is your view, the promises to Abraham provide a lens for seeing how God's faithfulness to provide land and preserve Israel point forward to a restoration of Israel in the land under Christ in the future.

Others argue that the promises of nationhood and land are temporary symbols ("types") that find *spiritual* fulfillment in Christ and the church (spiritual Israel) and *physical* fulfillment in an expanded "land," the new heaven and the new earth. If this is your view, the promises to Abraham make you alert to God's ultimate commitment of having a people with Abrahamic faith in Jesus in the new creation for all eternity.

*God's covenant at Sinai: Preparing a holy nation.* It is at Mount Sinai where the next phase of God's covenantal story of redemption unfolds. After delivering his people from slavery in Egypt, God meets with Moses and his people at Mount Sinai. Building on the fabric of the Abrahamic covenant, a new covenantal layer arises at Sinai where God now specifies how he expects Israel to live as a nation (Ex 19–24). The only difference in our triangular depiction of redemptive history in the Sinai covenant is the addition of "via obeying Torah" (see fig. 4.4). The Sinai covenant prepares God's people Israel to live in God's presence as a holy nation in the Promised Land through obeying his instructions. This will enable them to carry out the mission God intends for them, to be a blessing to all nations.

There are three key elements in the Sinai covenant:

- *Torah.* Torah is a Hebrew word that means "instruction." Much of Exodus–Deuteronomy contains instructions from God given at Sinai about how they are to live.

- *Nationhood.* God had commanded Abraham to live uprightly (Gen 17:1-2) and to promote justice (18:19), but now Israel's population is burgeoning and needs instruction about how to do this as a nation. They are about to inherit their land. It is time for God to specify how he expects Israel to live as a nation.

- *Holy King.* The Sinai covenant is often described as a suzerain-vassal treaty—a treaty between a powerful king (suzerain) and a people (vassal) who will live under the king's rule. Since God pledges to be in the midst of Israel, seated on the throne of the Ark of the Covenant as king, this requires careful instructions concerning how Israel is to behave in his holy presence. If Israel obeys, the king will bless them. If Israel disobeys, God will bring a curse on them in the land.

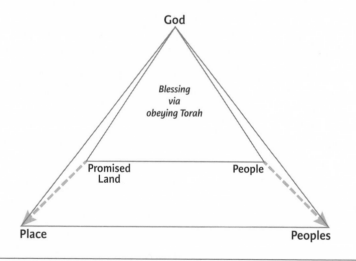

**Figure 4.4.** Covenant at Sinai: expectations for the nation

The key development that comes from the Sinai covenant is that Israel's experience of God's blessing (right side of inner triangle) in the land (left side of inner-triangle) will depend on their obedience to God's instruction (center of inner triangle).

*Reading in light of the Sinai covenant.* If God's mission to bless the world through a particular people (Israel) in a particular place (Canaan) depends on Torah obedience, then we must be alert to how God's law at Sinai informs our reading of the Scriptures.

As Moses anticipated (see Deut 31:24-29), Israel would disobey God's instructions. As we read Israel's story, we need to attune ourselves to see how Israel's disobedience regarding the Sinai covenant frustrates the fulfillment of God's promises to Israel. Although we see glimmers of obedience and blessing at times, Israel never fully experiences God's creation ideal of God's blessing in his presence in the Promised Land. As a result, in the pages of the Old Testament, Israel never becomes the channel of blessing for all nations anticipated in God's promises to Abraham, although there are glimpses of this when foreigners such as Rahab, the Gibeonites, and Ruth find blessing through aligning with Israel.

This history of failure in obeying the Sinai covenant culminates in exile, yet also prepares for Jesus. Jesus is born under the law of Sinai, and through his perfect obedience accomplishes what Israel could not. He fulfills the law and at the same time experiences the curses for disobedience, through crucifixion, warned about in the law, releasing Israel from the curse resulting from disobeying the specifications of the Sinai covenant (Gal 2–3). This ushers in an era where blessing flows through Jesus and his Jewish apostles to the rest of the world.

## GOING DEEPER: Law at Sinai and New Covenant Believers

It can be tricky to read the instructions given at Sinai as Christians. The church is not a nation, so how do instructions given to Israel on how to live as a nation relate to us? Jesus fulfills the expectations of and bears the curse of the Sinai covenant, so how should Christians read it today? Here are a few tips.

- God's law at Sinai teaches us about God and his desires for people. If God remains the same yesterday, today, and forever, then this means the Torah of Sinai shows us something true about who God is and what he wants from his people. Even if humanity fails to obey it, the *Torah* is still good. Yes, these laws were originally given to Israel as a nation, but the church can still learn from these good laws.

- The law illuminates Israel's repeated failures. We can ask how the Sinai covenant helps us see a recurring inability to obey God's commands.

- The Sinai covenant exposes our need for Jesus. Jesus comes to fulfill the expectations of the law and bear its curse. This opens the door for blessings to flow through Jesus to Jews and Gentiles.

As an example, consider Exodus 22:1 (see step two for more on Old Testament law): "If a man steals an ox or a sheep, and kills it or sells it, he shall repay five oxen for an ox, and four sheep for a sheep" (ESV). As a national law, Israel learns what is expected within their society. When cases arise where someone steals livestock and then kills or sells it, Israel knows how to handle it at a civic level. Since new covenant believers are no longer living as a nation in need of civil laws and prescribed punishments, our focus is on what this law reveals about God: stealing something and making it unreturnable should result in a restitution greater than what was taken. God wants us to honor the property of others; if we don't, a repayment of four or fivefold is in order.

Throughout Israel's story, we see kings and the powerful confiscating property with no repercussions. Jesus, however, came to bear the curse of the law while creating a new people who are to delight in what these laws reveal about God and allow this law to direct their steps. Our God desires that we honor the property of others, and, if we fail to do so, we should take measures to restore what was taken. Thank God there is forgiveness in Jesus and also the power of the Holy Spirit to help us grow toward obeying what God is revealing through his law at Sinai.

For further insight into how God's law at Sinai functions within the redemptive story of the Pentateuch, see Carmen Imes, *Bearing God's Name: Why Sinai Still Matters* (IVP Academic, 2019).

*God's covenant with David: Blessing through a king.* The covenant with Noah creates a stable context within which redemption could unfold, even as sin spreads like wildfire. God's covenants with Abraham and with Israel at Sinai reveal God's plan to save the world. He will bless the world through his people (Israel) as they experience God's blessing in the Promised Land through obeying the Sinai covenant. Now, in God's covenant with David, Davidic kingship emerges as the channel through which Israel and the world will experience God's blessing.

In 2 Samuel 7, David voices his desire to build God a house, a temple. God declines David's offer, yet offers a deal of his own.[3]

---

[3]Although the term *covenant* does not occur in 2 Sam 7, Ps 89 speaks of the episode as a covenant.

God will build David a house, a dynasty. God will relate with David's dynasty as a father relates to a son. God will never reject the Davidic dynasty, and a Davidic king would rule from David's throne forever. Through God's covenant with David, we gain yet another inner triangle (see fig. 4.5).

God's plan to work through a particular people, Israel, to bless all peoples (right side of triangles) narrows further to an individual Davidic king. As the representative of Israel who will lead the way in obeying God's instruction at Sinai, Davidic kingship becomes the channel of blessing for Israel and all nations (see Ps 72:17).

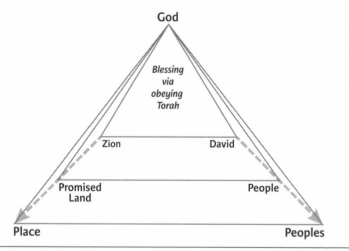

**Figure 4.5.** Covenant with David

The Davidic king also plays an important role in relationship to place. As is illustrated in the bottom left of our triangles, David establishes Zion (Jerusalem) as the capital in the Promised Land (2 Sam 6). Under his rule in Zion, now God will "provide a place for my people Israel" amidst the rule of Davidic kings (2 Sam 7:10). The promise of Abraham regarding land will find fulfillment under the rule of the Davidic king from Zion.

The general promises, then, concerning Abraham's offspring and land particularize in the line of the Davidic king and Zion. The Sinai covenant also remains in effect—the Davidic king would need to obey God's instructions if Israel (and the nations) is to experience God's blessing.

David now takes a central place in God's plans to restore his triangulated ideal for creation that is unraveling due to sin. With a Davidic king leading the way in obeying God's instructions, God's blessing would flow to Israel in the land and all nations across the earth.

*Reading in light of the Davidic covenant.* There are moments in the reigns of David and his son Solomon where Israel experiences God's blessing. Yet, David fails to obey the instructions of Sinai by committing adultery with Bathsheba and murdering her husband, Uriah. Solomon disobeys all of the expectations for a king as stated in Deuteronomy 17 by acquiring horses from Egypt, amassing gold, and marrying hundreds of foreign wives. More damning, Solomon ends up worshiping other gods.

After the nation divides in two (see step 3), over half of Judah's nineteen kings from the line of David "do evil in the eyes of the Lord," violating the Sinai covenant through idolatry. When the wickedness of the Davidic kings reaches its peak in Manasseh, God declares the unthinkable: God would allow Judah to be taken into exile, including the removal of the Davidic king from Jerusalem. In 586 BC, Jerusalem falls to Babylon and there has not been a ruler from the line of David on a throne in Jerusalem since.

During this time, God inspired his prophets to speak of a coming Davidic king whose rule would bring blessing to Israel and peace to the world forever (see Is 9:6-7; 11:1-9). Clinging to these promises, the faithful waited for the return of the king. The opening words of the New Testament identify Jesus as the awaited Messiah: "The genealogy of Jesus the Messiah the son of David, the son of Abraham" (Mt 1:1).

Jesus is not only from David's line, but he also fulfills the expectation of complete obedience to the law—something no Davidic king before him had accomplished. As we read with the Davidic covenant in view, we learn to be attentive to how Davidic kingship plays a central role in the outworking of God's plans to recover God's creation ideals through Israel.

*The new covenant in Jesus.* In the face of exile, one thing is clear: Israel and its kings are no better at obeying God's Word than Adam and Eve. Like Adam and Eve, Israel and its kings sin. Like Adam and Eve, Israel and its kings must leave the land as punishment. God's creation ideal of dwelling with an obedient people in a place continues to unravel. Does any hope remain?

The prophets boldly declare that God's redeeming love continues. Several of them speak of a "new covenant" that is on the horizon. By "new," this does not mean that it is disconnected or entirely different from the earlier redemptive covenants. The prophets have two elements of newness in view when they speak of the new covenant.

*New era of forgiveness.* Generation after generation in Israel broke the Sinai covenant. This mass of sin led to a massive rupture between God and his people. The only hope for restoration would depend on a new gift of forgiveness. God declares through Jeremiah that in the new covenant,

> I will forgive their wickedness
>> and will remember their sins no more. (Jer 31:34)

In Ezekiel, God says,

> I will sprinkle clean water on you, and you will be clean.
>> (Ezek 36:25)

In Isaiah, the new covenant era of forgiveness would come through a Suffering Servant:

> For he bore the sin of many,
>> and made intercession for the transgressors. (Is 53:12)

The prophets await a "new covenant" that would involve a new era of forgiveness made available through the Suffering Servant.

*New hearts that obey.* The problem with the Sinai covenant is not the laws themselves. The problem is sinful human hearts that break God's covenant. The prophets look forward to a time when God would transform hearts. God says in Jeremiah that he will write the law on their hearts (Jer 31:33). Ezekiel has a remarkable declaration of this: "And I will give you a new heart, and a new spirit I will put within you. And I will remove the heart of stone from your flesh and give you a heart of flesh. And I will put my Spirit within you, and cause you to walk in my statutes and be careful to obey my rules" (Ezek 36:26-27 ESV). God's Spirit will transform hearts in the new covenant so that God's people will be able to hear and obey his voice. Thus, at the heart of the new covenant is a new era of forgiveness and the transformation of hearts to obey.

*Reading in light of the new covenant.* Our triangulated depiction of God's redemptive story has one final addition: Jesus and the Holy Spirit (fig. 4.6). With the disobedience of the human heart and a need for forgiveness as barriers in God's mission to restore the ideals of creation, God sends his Son Jesus.

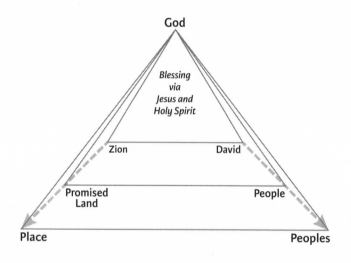

**Figure 4.6.** New covenant in Jesus

Jesus comes to Zion, the heart of the Promised Land, the capital of the entire world (left side of triangle). In an upper room in Zion, Jesus raises a glass of wine and says to his disciples, "This is my blood of the covenant, which is poured out for many for the forgiveness of sins" (Mt 26:28). When Jesus graces the table with these words, Jesus shows us that his own blood shed on the cross would flow in forgiveness for sins of Davidic kings, Israel, and all the peoples of the earth (right side of triangle). Sin creates an insurmountable gulf between God and people, and Jesus the Suffering Servant inaugurates a new covenant era with forgiveness.

The hope for hearts that obey also finds fulfillment, at least partially, in the new covenant era. When God pours out the Holy Spirit at Pentecost, a new level of knowing God becomes possible. God makes his home with us, and hard hearts that were unresponsive to God's voice begin beating again. New life sprouts, and the fruit of the Spirit springs forth in our lives. Slowly, but surely, our hearts begin flowing to the beat of love toward God and neighbor.

*Finalization of God's redemptive story.* Although we now live in the era of the new covenant, we await a greater realization of all of the covenants when Christ comes again, when the grand story of God's redeeming love reaches its conclusion.

Although death has ultimately been defeated in Jesus' death and resurrection, we still experience death. Although sin has been forgiven at the cross, we continue to succumb to temptation. Although we have access to God through faith in Christ, we long to see God face to face. Although we have hope in a new creation, we still live amid thorns and thistles.

Revelation 21 depicts the full realization of God's covenantal story to redeem his world—a world that has unraveled far from his ideal in creation. Check out how many themes from redemptive history surface in these four verses:

> Then I saw "a new heaven and a new earth," for the first heaven and the first earth had passed away, and there was no longer any sea. I saw the Holy City, the new Jerusalem, coming down out of heaven from God, prepared as a bride beautifully dressed for her husband. And I heard a loud voice from the throne saying, "Look! God's dwelling place is now among the people, and he will dwell with them. They will be his people, and God himself will be with them and be their God. 'He will wipe every tear from their eyes.

There will be no more death' or mourning or crying or pain,

for the old order of things has passed away." (Rev 21:1-4)

The triangulated ideal of God, people, and place is redeemed and then some. The world once cursed with thorns and thistles will become a "new heaven and new earth." The distance sin created between God and people will be vanquished, for "God's dwelling place is now among the people." Death too will be history.

And, so, the hopes from all the covenants that found a level of fulfillment in Christ's first coming will find their ultimate fulfillment when Christ comes again. What a beautiful story of redemption to recover God's presence among his people in a bountiful place.

If you would like to read further about God's redemptive story, I would recommend Sandra Richter's *The Epic of Eden* (IVP Academic, 2008) or Vaughn Roberts's *God's Big Picture* (InterVarsity Press, 2003). My use of triangles is inspired by a more academic treatment of God's story of redemption by Christopher Wright in *The Mission of God* (IVP Academic, 2006).

## SURFING THROUGH REDEMPTIVE HISTORY

I have never been successful at riding a surfboard, but I love bodyboarding. The key is to see a wave coming, catch the wave, and ride the wave in the direction it is heading.

Reading a passage in view of redemptive history is a lot like surfing. When you are studying a passage, you need to see how the wave is developing before it reaches your passage. This involves looking back at the prologue to redemption in Genesis 1–11 and the other covenants that come before your passage.

Next, you need to *catch the wave* in your passage. Usually, a passage will have a number of unique emphases that tap into specific elements in redemptive history, so this will give you focus points as you discern how a wave has been developing and where it is heading.

Finally, when you *ride a wave*, it does not always head directly to shore. Sometimes it flows left, right, or combines with another wave. With a grip on the uniqueness of your wave, take its unique path to Jesus' first and second comings.

Here is an example of surfing through redemptive history. Suppose you are studying the final verses of Exodus. God has delivered Israel out of Egypt. Israel has been meeting with God at Mount Sinai, and they just finished building God a tabernacle. At this important moment, with the tabernacle all set, we read, "Then the cloud covered the tent of meeting, and the glory of the LORD filled the tabernacle. Moses could not enter the tent of meeting because the cloud had settled on it, and the glory of the Lord filled the tabernacle" (Ex 40:34-35). How might we surf through redemptive history when reading this passage? *Seeing how the wave has been developing* invites me to look back to Genesis 1–3 and the covenants before Sinai, especially with regards to God's presence. In Genesis 2, Adam and Eve live in close proximity to God's special presence, but due to sin God casts them out of his presence when he kicks them out of Eden. In the covenant with Abraham, God promises to be uniquely present with him and his offspring. God appears via dreams and speaks to Abraham and his family on occasion, yet one wonders when and how God will again dwell amid humanity in the sort of close proximity Adam and Eve knew.

*Catching the wave* anchors us in what direction Exodus 40:34 is heading. At this monumental moment, God's special, glorious presence makes a home in the tabernacle at Sinai. Is this a recovery of what was lost when Adam and Eve left Eden? Is this the fulfillment of the hopes that God would be with Israel as he had been with Adam and Eve? Only in part. The glorious God of creation, now in covenant with Israel, is dwelling with humanity again in the tabernacle, but this is presence at a distance and is only ensured if Israel obeys the covenant. Moses cannot even enter the tabernacle. So this taste of recovering God's presence invites us to catch this wave and ride it further down the line of redemptive history.

*Riding the wave* of Exodus 40:34 results in a lengthy, yet beautiful journey. In the Davidic covenant, God states that Solomon would build a house for him. God's glorious presence fills Solomon's temple (1 Kings 8:10), but Israel's sin results in God punishing them by eventually destroying the temple. Hope remains, however, among the prophets that God would again dwell among his people. When Jesus came to earth, John declares, "The Word became flesh and made his dwelling among us. We have seen his glory" (Jn 1:14). How remarkable! The glorious presence of God that filled the tabernacle and temple came to inhabit human flesh. This, however, is not the end of the wave. We ride the wave into the age of the church, when God dwells in the church by the Holy Spirit. We await, however, a greater recovery of access to God's presence. In John's vision in Revelation 21, he sees a new heaven and a new earth. In this vision, an angel announces, "Look! God's dwelling place is now among the people, and he will dwell with them" (Rev 21:3).

By surfing the wave of redemptive history, we come to see how Exodus 40:34 is part of a much larger story. This is a redemptive story where God restores his presence with his people by taking on flesh in Jesus, filling the church by the Holy Spirit, and ultimately in the second coming when God dwells with us in a way that goes far beyond what Adam and Eve even experienced.

## CONCLUSION

By way of conclusion, imagine that you are an art student and walk into a classroom with sixty-five other students. The teacher gives you each a tile with unique instructions about how you are to design that tile. One by one the teacher calls you up and asks you to describe your tile to the class. You then hand your tile to the teacher who places your tile in a strategic spot on a board covered with plaster. After you all present and the teacher sets each piece strategically, the teacher holds up a beautiful mosaic. All sixty-six tiles are now fit together as a single work of art. This can be an analogy for the Bible.

As we study the Bible, we need not study only individual tiles (steps 2 and 3). We also need to see how all sixty-six tiles create a beautiful whole. In "Step 4: Whole Bible," I've offered two ways to consider how a passage fits within the mosaic: (1) look for parallels between what your passage teaches about God and what we see in Jesus; (2) surf across redemptive history by identifying a wave's development, catching the wave, and riding it home. Enjoy the ride!

## DISCUSSION QUESTIONS

1. Have you seen any helpful or unhelpful ways that some can find Jesus in the Old Testament? What are they?

2. Using Psalm 23 or a favorite Old Testament passage, answer this question: What does this passage say about God, and how is this reflected in Jesus? What do you find?

3. How do the two parameters in figural reading help you evaluate the validity of how Psalm 23 points to Jesus?

4. What did you find most helpful or most confusing about the sketch of redemptive history? In what ways were the triangles helpful or confusing?

5. How would you answer this question if a middle school student asked you: How does Jesus fulfill the Old Testament covenants?

*Step 5*

# Savor God

THREE YEARS AGO, I BECAME A PESCATARIAN for health reasons. The only meat I eat is fish (except on holidays). When you have a weird diet, you find yourself cooking food that you don't end up eating. Family and friends gather. I work my magic on the grill. They plate up juicy burgers, seasoned chicken, and plump hotdogs. And then, there is me. The Chef. Not savoring any of the grilled goodies.

This can be a parable for my journey in studying God's Word. I often settle for cooking a great meal yet never taste it. When I first began reading God's Word, I felt so close to God. Then I started thinking more strategically about how to read the Bible. Through classes in college, seminary, and grad school, my skills in literary, historical, and canonical analysis grew. But something else was growing—a gap between me and God.

I could write essays, preach sermons, and deliver lectures on what a passage means in its original (steps 2–3) and whole Bible (step 4) contexts. After all, the aim of most academic classes and books on how to read the Bible was to write an essay or preach. My growth in analysis led to paralysis in my relationship with God. I became skilled at cooking up savory meats, but did not savor them.

I am not alone in this. A highly respected New Testament scholar named Daniel Wallace shared his own experience. One of his sons was diagnosed with a rare form of kidney cancer. In that moment, Wallace needed God, not just another round of textual analyses. Wallace writes, "I found a longing to get closer to God, but found myself unable to do so through my normal means: exegesis, Scripture reading, more exegesis. I believe that I had depersonalized God so much that when I really needed him I didn't know how to relate."[1]

I see the same thing year after year among my college students. They sense a drift amid their academic study, a depersonalization with the God of the Bible as they analyze the Good Book. They are in danger of becoming master chefs that never taste the food. Their growing concern is how to stay close to God amid their academic studies.

Step five invites us beyond cooking to tasting the goodness of God through Scripture.

## THE GOAL OF BIBLE STUDY

Steps one, five, and six in this book stem from my own journey to bridge the gap. I have fought and continue to fight tooth and nail against the forces in the academy that push us to keep the Bible at arm's length for the sake of scientific objectivity. Folks. We are not neutral observers who coolly examine ancient texts.

Listen to how the psalmist in Psalm 119 speaks of his engagement with the Bible:

I have hidden your word in my heart. (Ps 119:11)
I reach out for your commands, which I love,

---

[1]Daniel B. Wallace, "Who's Afraid of the Holy Spirit?," *Christianity Today*, September 12, 1994.

that I may meditate on your decrees. (Ps 119:48)

Your decrees are the theme of my song. (Ps 119:54)

The psalmist is anything but a neutral observer of God's Word.

Our aim is not simply to know our Bibles better. Our ultimate goal is not simply to figure out what a passage means in light of its ancient context. Our purpose is not even to wax eloquently about how a passage relates to Jesus and fits into the whole story of the Bible.

What, then, should our aim be? J. I. Packer captures it well: "[The true joy in reading the Bible] is the deep contentment that comes of communing with the living Lord into whose presence the Bible takes us."[2] The aim of reading the Bible is communing with the living Lord, a communion that results in worship, repentance, healing, and obedience (see step 6).

The Bible is a means, not the end. Yes, we want to rightly interpret God's Word (2 Tim 2:15), but right interpretation of the Bible is not our ultimate aim. The Bible is a channel through which the Holy Spirit encounters us, opening our hearts to see God, drawing us near through Jesus, transforming us, and making us more aware of God's presence. Our aim is to meet with and hear from God through the Scriptures.

The truth of the matter is that step five, along with step six, should be interwoven across the entire process of reading the Bible. You are allowed to savor God throughout all of the steps as you read God's Word! There can be a benefit, though, in being intentional about savoring God toward the end of the interpretative process. In step five, we turn to savor God.

---

[2]J. I. Packer, *God Has Spoken: Revelation and the Bible*, 3rd ed. (Grand Rapids, MI: Baker Books, 1993), 16.

## LECTIO DIVINA

What does it mean to savor God as we read Scripture? To answer this question, let me introduce an ancient approach to reading Scripture called *lectio divina*. *Lectio* is Latin for "reading" and *divina* for "divine" or "spiritual." *Lectio divina* is spiritual reading, reading that brings you into communion with the divine. Its formulation stems from Saint Benedict (AD 480–547), an Italian monk whose rules for his monastery turned into a global movement of spiritual formation. There are at least four elements involved in a divine, spiritual reading of the Bible.

- *Lectio* is the reading or study of the Scriptures. Much of what we covered in steps two, three, and four fits into *lectio*. Sure God can speak to us through an uninformed reading of a passage; God can graciously do that. However, a spiritual reading of the Bible that does not include a careful reading of the Bible could fall into the danger of separating Spirit from truth. A close reading of the Bible (steps 2 through 4) can be as important to a spiritual reading as a skeleton is to a body.

*Spiritual formation* is a branch of academic study that carefully considers how religious people experience transformation and encounter God. Unfortunately, training in spiritual formation and training in biblical exegesis rarely intertwine, as they are considered separate disciplines academically. My hope is that the two can mutually enrich one another.

- *Meditatio* is meditation. For some, meditation calls to mind a Buddhist monk who seeks to empty their mind, but biblical meditation is different. Biblical meditation keeps the mind fully engaged through the Spirit by mulling over, gnawing on, and digesting God's Word. This is reflected in Psalm 1's "blessed" person "whose delight is in the law of the Lord, and who meditates on his law day and night" (Ps 1:2). Meditation does not just happen during a quiet moment. You can chew on God's Word throughout your entire day, yearning to glean more and more honey from Scripture.

- *Oratio* is prayer. We should pray before, during, and in response to our Bible reading. This fuels fellowship with God as one engages God's Word. Psalm 119 offers many windows into the psalmist's desire to hear from God through his Word. I love this prayer: "Open my eyes that I may see wonderful things in your law" (Ps 119:18). Prayer can take many forms, such as requests for God's illumination, praise to God in view of what God is revealing about himself, naming specifics in your life or the world, or honest questions for God.

- *Contemplatio* is contemplation. The idea is to be still, allowing the Holy Spirit to draw you into God's presence through the Word. It occurs at the moment you gain a glimpse of God and his truth, and you choose to simply rest in this. In Psalm 119, yearning for God's presence intertwines with the repeated emphasis on God's Word. So the psalmist says, "You are my portion, Lord; I have promised to obey your words. I have sought your face with all my heart" (Ps 119:57-58). Being in the Word stems from a desire to bask in God's presence.

Reading. Meditation. Prayer. Contemplation. These are not steps in a process, but elements in Bible reading that intertwine, like a braid. These four elements of *lectio divina* bring us to the heart of Bible reading: prayerful (*oratio*) study (*lectio*) that seeps into our heart (*meditatio*) and draws us into communion with God (*contemplatio*).

> *Lectio divina* brings us to the heart of Bible reading:
> prayerful (*oratio*) study (*lectio*) that seeps into
> our heart (*meditatio*) and draws us into communion
> with God (*contemplatio*).

## ENJOYING GOD THROUGH THE WORD

As noted above, prayer, meditation, and contemplation should intertwine throughout your study of the Bible as you go about steps one, two, three, and four. Yet, tremendous benefit can come from a prayerful and meditative rereading of your passage after these steps. By the time you finish step four, you have gathered a lot of wood and kindling. Now it is time to enjoy the blazing campfire. An intentional moment of reflection will provide space to enjoy the light, heat, and smells of God's Word by the power of the Holy Spirit.

In step five, prayer, meditation, and contemplation weave together as you go back through the passage. Prayerfully and slowly move verse-by-verse or subunit-by-subunit through the passage after completing step four. Beginning with the first verse or subunit, you might find that the following intertwining flow works for you:

- Pray for illumination (similar to step 1) that God will help you see what a verse or subunit of verses is saying about him. Ask God to reveal what he wants you to see about himself at this particular moment in time. (*oratio*)

- Meditate by chewing on each word and each line, letting the flow of these words that you grasped in step two sink into you in a personal way and looking for what may stand out. (*meditatio*)

- Praise God in response to the glimpses you see of him. (*oratio*)

- Prayerfully bring what is most pressing from your life to God and wrestle with God about what you find difficult in a passage. (*oratio*)

- Chew on the passage a bit more, listening for God to speak to specifics in your life. (*meditatio*)

- Bask in his presence. Let yourself just "be" with such a wondrous God. (*contemplatio*)

You will know when to move on to the next verse or subunit, again prayerfully inviting the Holy Spirit to help you see God, chewing on his Word, praising him, and resting in him.

As you see, step five builds on your analyses in steps two, three, and four, yet it pushes us beyond analysis to savoring the God who was and is and is to come. To savoring the God who is not just an idea in the text but the living, triune God who is active in our world today and desires fellowship with us. To savoring a God who wants to reveal himself to us and speak to us in the here and now.

## EXAMPLES

My first experiences with step five came through praying the Psalms. I would start by studying the psalm to have a sense for what it is saying and where it is heading (step 2). Then I would go back through the psalm, allowing it to direct my prayers to God and guide me into his presence.

Step five will look different for everyone. Our own unique personalities and experiences will flavor our prayers, meditations, and contemplations. God will reveal himself and address us all in different ways, as our good Father knows what we each need in each moment. Nevertheless, our understandings of Scripture stemming from steps two through four should remain the backbone that directs our *lectio divina*.

To offer a sense of what *lectio divina* looks like, here are examples from Psalm 121 and Ephesians 2, passages we considered in step two. Any worked example will naturally be artificial. At different times in our lives, the Holy Spirit will speak to us differently from the same passage due to our life circumstances. You can view these examples as prompts for prayerful engagement with God through his Word.

***Psalm 121.*** A Song of Ascent

*Oh God, I journey with my sisters and brothers in the psalms of ascent to meet with you. Open my eyes by the power of the Holy Spirit that I might see your wonders in Christ.*

Psalm 121:1-2, My Helper Made Heaven and Earth.

I lift up my eyes to the mountains—
    where does my help come from?
My help comes from the LORD,
    the Maker of heaven and earth.

*I lift my eyes to you. Oh, how I need you. You know the trials I am in. The ancients thought the gods dwelt on mountains, so this is where they looked for help. Yet, you are not confined to mountains. You sit enthroned in the heavens, with your Son beside you, your Son whose hands still bear the marks of nails. My world may be falling apart, but you made all things and are not surprised or threatened. I turn to you.*

*I sense spiritual warfare as I write this chapter, Lord. The evil one accuses saying, "Who are you to write a chapter on spiritual reading!" Where Oh Lord does my help come from?*

*I claim today this truth—that you, Yahweh, are my help. You are not just a local god. You are the personal, covenant God of Israel, of my family in Christ. You are the maker of heaven and earth. Help me to know this in the very fiber of my being!* [pause to praise God and bask in the knowledge of God as Maker of heaven and earth]

*How wondrous is it that you are a God we can look to! How is it that I can consider you "my helper"?! How splendid that Jesus declared that you would send us the Helper, the Holy Spirit! Would you help me in this moment?*

*I rest in you, my help.* [moment of resting contemplation, reminded by the Holy Spirit that Christ overcame the evil one and that the gospel of grace should be my confidence]

Psalm 121:3-4, Our Keeper Does Not Sleep.

He will not let your foot slip—
 he who watches over you will not slumber;
indeed, he who watches over Israel
 will neither slumber nor sleep.

*Father, it says, "He will not let your foot slip." I admit that I struggle to make sense of this. I feel like your people and I often slip. The psalmist certainly knew that Israel had fallen many, many times. Perhaps people in crisis benefit from clear-cut promises like this, without qualification? Perhaps it is beneficial to have an orientation of hope amid trial? Is this more of an ultimate promise, that ultimately God's church will be kept safe forever in Christ?*

*Maybe I need to stop overanalyzing and just receive this good, gracious word: you will not let my foot slip. You know the mountain I am climbing in the short term and long term. You know how off balance I get. Please keep watch over me, Lord, that I might not slip and fall.*

*How glorious it is that you don't sleep! You watch over me and your people without taking a break, without even a little catnap. I cling to this truth, but I again struggle to see this. Your church is ravaged. Some of your faithful face attacks, bombings, and arrests simply for bearing your name. Some fall into grave sin, as scandal after scandal comes to light. Yet, Jesus, you declared that you would build your church. Your church is a blood-bought gift. I affirm my trust that you are watching and will watch over her to the end, without sleeping.* [pause for contemplation]

Psalm 121:5-6, Your Keeper is Your Shade.

> The LORD watches over you—
>> the LORD is your shade at your right hand;
> the sun will not harm you by day,
>> nor the moon by night.

*Oh, Lord it keeps coming up—you watch over us. Impress this truth on my heart. Let this sink into my bones. For I again wrestle with this. Lord, help me. I can be so skeptical and analytical. You know I just read Acts 7, when your servant Stephen died through stoning. You know I just read about the early martyr Perpetua who died for her faith. I think too of your faithful innocents who died in El Salvador when Oscar Romero was priest. Were you their shade?*

*Your own Son, though, experienced grave suffering too. Even as he died, he entrusted himself to your care. You resurrected and exalted him. And ultimately through Jesus' death and resurrection, you were indeed watching over me and all of your people. You overcame the most ultimate harm through Jesus—sin, death, and the evil one. I praise you Lord. Be my shade.* [pause for contemplation on God as my shade]

Psalm 121:7-8, God Keeps You Forever.

The LORD will keep you from all harm—
> he will watch over your life;
the LORD will watch over your coming and going
> both now and forevermore.

*How wondrous is it that you, Lord, are mindful of every aspect of my life. When I go pick up my daughter from camp, when I write this book, when I do the dishes, when I feel anxious, and when Katie and I make plans, you are keeping watch. You, Lord, knew that I needed Psalm 121 today. I praise you for renewing my confidence that you, the maker of heaven and earth, are watching out for me, even as I sense warfare.*

[take a moment to just "be" in the presence of our keeper]

As you can see in this example from Psalm 121, meditation, prayer, and contemplation intermingle in step five. I am chewing on God's Word throughout, allowing its flow and words to provide direction. My prayers range from requests for illumination, praises for who God is, and honest questions. Contemplation usually is the byproduct of chewing on the Word and prayer. Finally, notice how I did not separate my current moment and experiences from the process—God wants us to come as we are so he can minister to us and uniquely dazzle us with glimpses of himself.

Naturally, any written example of *lectio divina* is artificial, for the living God acts freely as he meets with his people through the Word. It is also difficult to articulate the meditation and contemplation sides of the process. God may speak differently to each of us at different times from the same passage, so the examples are simply illustrative.

Why don't you go ahead and pick a short psalm and try it yourself? Begin with a brief time of finding its flow (step 2) and then move verse-by-verse or subunit-by-subunit back through in a prayerful, meditative, and contemplative fashion.

*Ephesians 2:1-10.* It is perhaps easy to imagine doing *lectio divina* with a psalm because it is already a prayer. But what about other parts of Scripture? *Lectio divina* is suitable for everywhere in God's Word. *Lectio divina* is really all about engaging with God in a personal way through his Word. Sure, this will look different depending on the type of passage you are studying, its content, your own life circumstances, and the free movement of the Spirit, but the aim is the same: to meet with God.

Let's consider Ephesians 2:1-10 as a way of illustrating *lectio divina* outside the Psalms. We will move subunit-by-subunit (see the analysis of Eph 2 in step 2).

Ephesians 2:1-3, All Were Dead in the Sinful Course of the World.

As for you, you were dead in your transgressions and sins, in which you used to live when you followed the ways of this world and of the ruler of the kingdom of the air, the spirit who is now at work in those who are disobedient. All of us also lived among them at one time, gratifying the cravings of our flesh and following its desires and thoughts. Like the rest, we were by nature deserving of wrath.

*Father, by the Holy Spirit, open my eyes to see your wonders in this passage. Meet me where I am and draw me deeper into the love of Jesus.*

*In all honesty, I do not regularly think of myself and other brothers and sisters as having been dead. Remind me of this! Help the gravity of this sink in, Lord.* [I meditate on my former course of life before I became a Christian at around age 11, and I also ponder the death I felt in my soul during a season of extreme rebellion from ages 16–20.]

*Like Adam and Eve before me, sin indeed leads to death. Your wrath is truly what I deserve. Help me to see all as either currently dead or formerly dead in sin.* [pause to contemplate having been or being dead in sin and deserving of wrath]

Ephesians 2:4-7, In Love and Grace, God Made us Alive in Christ.

But because of his great love for us, God, who is rich in mercy, made us alive with Christ even when we were dead in transgressions—it is by grace you have been saved. And God raised us up with Christ and seated us with him in the heavenly realms in Christ Jesus, in order that in the coming ages he might show the incomparable riches of his grace, expressed in his kindness to us in Christ Jesus.

*I praise you, Lord. We were truly dead and deserving of wrath, but thank you for your love for us. Yes, your love is for me, but your love is also for all of my brothers and sisters. How vast and wide and deep is your love. I praise you that my hope is not in myself; on my own, I'm dead in sin! Thank you, thank you for your love and rich mercy for dead sinners like me.* [pause to rest in God's love for dead sinners]

*The truth that you have made me alive, resurrected me, and seated me with Jesus in heaven is far beyond anything I can comprehend. I praise you. It is so, so hard to imagine myself in heaven right now, seated with your Son! Even more, it is hard to imagine all of your children there with you. Yet, you declare this. Expand my imagination and help my heart take this in.* [meditate on, praise God, and rest in the identity of being made alive, risen, and ascended with Christ]

Ephesians 2:8-10, Saved by Grace (not Works) for Good Works.

For it is by grace you have been saved, through faith—and this is not from yourselves, it is the gift of God—not by works, so that no one can boast. For we are God's handiwork, created in Christ Jesus to do good works, which God prepared in advance for us to do.

*I confess, Lord, that I drift into viewing good works as the way I keep you happy. If I serve the vulnerable, don't get angry with my kids, or am consistent in prayer and devotions, I tend to think I am right with you, God. Like an athlete trying to please a coach,*

*I mistakenly approach you as one I've kept happy with my performance.*

*But oh, the freeing and glorious truth that my ability to be with you has nothing to do with my works—salvation is a gift from you through Jesus! Work this truth into the very fiber of my being.* [pause to rest in God's grace]

*Father, I come to you open handed—it says that you've created me to live completely different from before when I was dead and walking according to the evil one. What are those good works you've created me to do in Christ Jesus? I am your vessel today, ready to step into what you have prepared for me. Help me to also see how my brothers and sisters are walking into the good works you have for them.* [with a posture of open hands, I rest in the truth of the entire passage—that the dead are made alive in Christ for good works in the world]

From this example with Ephesians 2:1-10, you again see the intersection of chewing on God's Word, praying to God in light of it, and taking moments to let these truths sink in and to enjoy God's presence.

I have illustrated *lectio divina* with a Psalm and a letter, but all other genres are worthy of prayerful, meditative engagement. In fact, the psalmist in Psalm 1 and Psalm 119 especially has law and perhaps narrative in mind. A biblical story, such as the one about Abram and Sarai, would lead us to savor God's intervention and wrestle with the degradation of Sarai before God. A law, such as the first commandment ("You shall have no other gods before me," Ex 20:2), invites us to savor God's worthiness of exclusive devotion in a world of competing gods.

## ADVICE

Now that you have a sense for the basics of *lectio divina*, I want
to offer three words of advice.

*Let your analysis in steps two through four provide direc-
tion and boundaries for step five.* God inspired his Word to have
a flow that would be understood in context and in light of Christ.
If we fail to allow our careful study to fuel our savoring of God,
we are in danger of inventing meanings and of denying the
incarnational character of God's Word. Sure, God can speak to
us however he wishes, but a careful reading of a passage is certainly what we should strive for. This will direct our engagement
with God in a way that protects from missteps.

*Be alert to when a community is in view in a passage.* Naturally, *lectio divina* requires that we engage personally with God
through his Word. This does not mean we are to be individualistic. As someone from an individualist society, it is easy for me
to turn *we/us* into *I/me*. If God's Word has a community in view,
we should engage with God personally in view of his desires for
the community. In Psalm 121, God is both the keeper of you and
of Israel. In Ephesians 2, "all of us" are dead in sin and objects of
wrath, God "loved us" and "made us alive," and God prepared
works "for us to do." Although *lectio divina* will naturally be very
personal, allow God's Word to invite us to see his heart for the
people of God as a whole too.

*Expect gradual transformation rather than ecstasy when
meditating.* We can sometimes assume that a "spiritual" reading
will always result in a rapturous journey into God's presence. We
expect fireworks. The Holy Spirit can certainly do this, yet the
norm seems to be for God to meet with us more subtly. More like

God's whisper to Elijah (1 Kings 19:12) than the fire of Pentecost (Acts 2). Don't be discouraged if you don't have an experience worthy of a TikTok or Instagram post. God grows his people gradually so we develop faithfulness and deep roots. God's gives us tastes of his presence, yet he keeps us hungry for the day we will see him face to face.

## CONCLUSION

Step five invites us into the ancient practice of *lectio divina*. Building on a strong grasp of Scripture from the first four steps, we incorporate meditation, prayer, and contemplation. The aim is to engage personally with God through the Bible by prayerfully allowing God's Word to seep into our pores and anchor us in God's presence. We push beyond the danger of analysis paralysis to a living God who wishes to meet with us through our study.

## DISCUSSION QUESTIONS

1. How has this chapter or this book changed, challenged, or enriched your motivations on why you read the Bible?

2. Can you remember a time when the Holy Spirit spoke powerfully to you through a passage of Scripture? Describe that experience.

3. *Lectio divina* involves *slowing down* as we read, meditate, and pray through Scripture. This kind of slowing is difficult to achieve in our fast-paced culture. What makes slowing down most difficult for you? Where in your daily life can you find the space to prioritize this?

4. Using Psalm 23, practice *lectio divina*, remembering not to neglect steps two through four. Describe your experience.

What was difficult? What was good? In what ways did the Holy Spirit speak to you?

5. Although we have been trained in our culture to expect immediate gratification or results, the practice of meditating on Scripture requires practice and discipline. Do not be discouraged if at first you feel weird and do not have deep insights. Spend a few minutes in prayer, share your thoughts honestly with God, and ask the Lord to encourage and empower you on this journey.

*Step 6*

# Faithful Response

AS I WRITE, CRISTIANO RONALDO—a famous soccer (football) player—has the most followers on Instagram at 406 million. Leading the way on Twitter is former US President Barack Obama at 131 million followers. There are lots and lots of followers out there.

If social media existed at the start of Jesus' ministry, he would have been trending. He's healing people left and right. He's declaring the kingdom of God. Folks from north and south are flocking to him. In fact, Matthew tells us, "Large crowds from Galilee, the Decapolis, Jerusalem, Judea and the region across the Jordan followed him" (Mt 4:25). Did you catch that last part? Large crowds are following Jesus; he has followers. Lots of them. The carpenter turned rabbi from Nazareth is trending.

Amid this surge in popularity, Jesus takes a seat on a mountainside and preaches the most famous sermon ever—the Sermon on the Mount (Mt 5–7). There are so many riches in this sermon, but I want to focus on how Jesus concludes it. This conclusion shows that Jesus puts little stock in amassing followers and likes; he seeks followers that obey.

Jesus' finale starts with an analogy: "Therefore everyone who hears these words of mine and puts them into practice is like a wise man who built his house on the rock" (Mt 7:24). Jesus points to the stuff of everyday life, building houses and foundations. Whoever hears his words *and* puts them into practice is like someone building a home on a rock. When rain pours, streams flood, and winds blast, the house will not fall because of its foundation—rock. To draw out his point, Jesus points to the inverse: "But everyone who hears these words of mine and does not put them into practice is like a foolish man who built his house on sand" (Mt 7:26). The difference between the wise and the fool boils down to whether they put Jesus' words into practice. Both the fool and the wise hear Jesus' words, but only the wise respond faithfully to them. The wise will withstand the storms, but the house of the fool will crash.

Jesus has little interest in setting records for followers. Anyone can click a heart, select "follow," and join a crowd. Jesus knows that some, perhaps many, will not put what they are hearing into practice; their houses will be built on sand and come crashing down. Yet some will respond faithfully to what they hear; their houses will be built on rock.

In step six, we strive to be the sort of followers Jesus seeks— those who respond faithfully to God's Word.

## TEMPLATE FOR RESPONDING FAITHFULLY

Throughout all of our steps, God has already been transforming us and inviting us to faithfully respond to his voice. Now we intentionally take stock of this. In step five, we began responding to God by praising him, praying to him, and delighting in him through the Word. In step six, we intentionally ask: What would a faithful response to God's voice look like in our daily lives?

A faithful response to God's voice through the Bible stems from the intersection of three dynamics: the Holy Spirit, the Bible, and you in real life (fig. 6.1). You come as you are to read the Bible, and God speaks through the Bible to minister to you in real life, amid all of the joys and difficulties in the world.

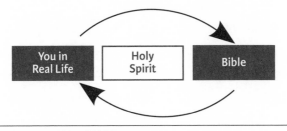

**Figure 6.1.** Dynamics within a faithful response

At the center of figure 6.1 is the Holy Spirit. Without the Holy Spirit, you and the Bible are sitting on opposite sides of a silent ballroom. When the Holy Spirit enters the room, music plays through the Bible, and you are able to dance in step with the Holy Spirit. The Holy Spirit draws you to the Bible, helps you hear its music, and directs you as you dance in your everyday life. This process happens over and over again.

The Holy Spirit works to bring us to a faithful response to God's Word in at least three ways.

- *Illumination.* God's glory and voice are sounding forth everywhere, in creation and in Scripture (see Ps 19). Yet, we do not see him and hear it. Our minds and hearts are darkened. We need the Holy Spirit to shine light on our hearts and minds to enable us to hear and see what God is communicating through the Word of God.

- *Personalization.* The Holy Spirit knows the specific circumstances in our lives and world, so the Holy Spirit will connect what God aims to communicate through the Bible with our current life circumstances and the needs of the world. The personalization of God's Word through the Holy Spirit will promote within you a sense of how God wishes for you to respond in your life, including conviction of sin and a summons to repent.

- *Empowerment.* Even if you know what a faithful response involves, we need the Holy Spirit to transform us and give us the power to respond faithfully to God's Word.

Although there can be many paths for moving toward a faithful response in conjunction with the Holy Spirit and the Bible, here is a sample sequence of what step six might look like in practice.

1. Prayer of dependence on the Holy Spirit for illumination, personalization, and empowerment.

2. Drawing on insights from steps two through four, revisit your passage and ask, "What is the main response(s) the human author would have desired from the original audience?"

3. With a grasp of what response the Word is calling for, ask God to help you see what this looks like in your own life. Come as you are—alert to weighty circumstances, sins, relationships, local and global challenges, and more.

4. In the power of the Holy Spirit, respond faithfully to what God is calling you to do, be, or see through his Word.

This four-part sequence honors the role of the Holy Spirit, while prioritizing the intentions of the Bible and acknowledging God's ability to speak through the Bible to our everyday lives.

Over the years, I have heard a few different "best ways" to read the Bible.

*Speech-act theory* describes how authors seek to do something with their words. When someone speaks, the words (locutions) are fashioned for a purpose (illocution), such as to warn, promise, describe, or bless, and a speaker usually hopes for a specific response from the listener (perlocutionary intent). If we want to respond faithfully to God's Word, then an essential step is to ponder how the original author would want a reader to respond to what they say.

Some say that the best way to read the Bible is on your knees, in prayer. Others say that the best way to read the Bible is with the Bible in one hand and the newspaper in the other, pondering how God's Word speaks to our world. Still others, especially in the last century, say that the best way to read the Bible is by figuring out what the original human author intended.

I see no reason to disconnect these "best ways" of reading the Bible. We can depend on the Holy Spirit. We can listen for how God addresses our lives and world through the Word. We can carefully study the Word to decipher God's aims in a passage. Through all of these together, we can come to know the steps of the dance God is inviting us into within our daily lives.

*An example: Acts 28.* Let me give a personal example. Recently, I finished the book of Acts, having read a chapter each day. When I reached Acts 28, I was struck by the noticeable lack of resolution it brings at the close of the book. It ends with Paul in Rome, under house arrest, with Jews rejecting the gospel and Paul shifting his attention to the Gentiles.

After prayer and careful study, I pondered: *How would the author of Acts expect readers to respond to Acts 28?* At one level, Luke certainly wants to *inform* his audience of how a small sect of Jews in Jerusalem grew to become a predominantly non-Jewish (Gentile) church that reached even to Rome. A faithful response for original readers would be to be informed about the spread of the church and the inclusion of Jews and Gentiles.

At another level, the open-ended nature of Acts 28 invites readers to *join in the mission* of witnessing to Jesus. The sense is that the word will continue to expand beyond Rome to reach even more Jews and Gentiles. A faithful response is to participate in this mission until Jesus comes again on the clouds of heaven.

As I invited God to help me see what a faithful response would look like in my circumstances, I was compelled simply to pray, "God, I am yours. Help me join your mission of reaching others. Help me see when you are orchestrating moments for me to witness to Jesus."

Later that day, I entered my bank to meet with an agent. My plans were to get a signature and leave. But God opened a door. The agent saw that my shirt said "Wheaton College" and asked if I worked there. Then she said these words: "So, do you believe in God?" Gulp. I wasn't expecting that. God is opening a door. I prayed: "Okay, Lord. Help me step into this. Give me the words to say." "Yes," I said. "I do believe in God."

My brief answer gave her an opening to share her doubts. She is having a hard time believing in God. There is so much evil in the world. Why doesn't God do anything about it? After she shared her thoughts, I stepped through the door to witness to Jesus. I shared about how we all do evil, and that God will judge all evil one day. The great news is that Jesus forgives evil people like me through his death, and hopefully is transforming his people to become agents of his love rather than evil.

I don't share this story to impress you. My words were not perfect. This banker did not come to Jesus in that moment. My sense, however, is that God had used Acts 28 to prepare me for this encounter. Our template (fig. 6.1) aims to show that as we study God's Word, the Holy Spirit gives us understanding (illumination), personalizes (personalization) the message of the Bible, and empowers us to respond faithfully amid the unique circumstances of our lives. I trust God will do the same for you.

Ask God to help you hear his voice. Ponder what a faithful response to God's Word might have involved for an original audience. Invite God to show you what a response would look like in the real circumstances of your life and world. Take action accordingly by the power of the Holy Spirit. Let God's Word set the agenda and invite the Holy Spirit to speak through it to the particulars of your life.

## FAITHFUL RESPONSE

With a template now in place for responding faithfully to God's Word, I want to expand on this. I want us to see that a faithful response involves more than *doing*; it also includes *being* and *seeing*. If what follows begins to feel a bit too complicated, please know that the last thing I want to do is make responding to God's voice complicated. If that is you, just focus on the guidance above.

Let's begin with why I frame step six as "faithful response" rather than "application."

"Application" is a popular term in Christian circles. In small group Bible study, the main question is often, "How does this apply to us?" Pastors will inevitably transition in their sermons to ask, "So, how does this apply to us?" Books on how to study or preach the Bible will present "application" as the final step in the process. My beef with "application" is that it is just so impersonal, human-centered, and detached from God's Word. This is not a hill that I'd die on, but I do prefer "faithful response" over "application."

What would happen if in Bible study we moved away from saying, "So how do we apply this to our lives?" What if instead we asked, "How might we respond faithfully to what God is saying?"

I posed a similar question on social media. By far, the strongest sentiment was that a shift from "application" to "faithful response" will help us become more God-centered rather than human-centered.

The logic beneath "application" is that a gap exists between us and the Bible, so we need to figure out what the ancient text meant back in the day and then come up with a parallel for how the ancient text might be applicable today. Throughout this application process, the Bible begins to feel like an ancient relic stuck in the past; it is up to trained exegetes to mine these ancient texts and figure out what remains applicable today.

I agree that there is a time gap between when the Bible was written and today, but there is more—a living God who speaks. What if God is personally speaking as we study and meditate on his Word? If God is really at work through his "living and active Word" (Heb 4:12), then wouldn't "faithful response" better capture that we are really responding to a person, to God? We are not just examining a text and taking it on ourselves to figure out its relevance. The aim of step six is to respond to the voice of the living God who speaks through the Word today.

*The eyeglasses of faith.* As we flesh out the being and seeing contours of a faithful response, the idea of the Bible as the "spectacles of faith" (John Calvin) can help us see how transformation and vision are integral parts of a faithful response.

When my oldest, Anna, was three, there was an eye screening event at our local library. It just so happened that my wife and daughter were there that day. On a whim, my wife made our exuberant daughter sit down for a quick screening. A machine scanned her eyes and printed out the results: the left eye does not refract light properly.

Of course, the rotary members hosting the event had no clue what this meant, so they just said that we should contact an eye doctor as soon as possible. At our doctor's appointment, she explained what was going on. One of Anna's eyes was becoming dominant, so her weaker eye was falling out of use. The solution would be simple: eyeglasses.

I was curious, though. Isn't there something more they should do for my daughter than have her wear glasses to help her see? Glasses, I assumed, would do nothing to fix her eye that was weaker. It turns out that I was wrong.

Anna began to wear cute, indestructible pink frames. Each lens had a different prescription, and the doctor would tweak the prescriptions every six months or so. Eventually, it dawned on me: these glasses not only helped Anna see better, but they also were rewiring the neural networks between her brain and eyes. Glasses not only helped Anna see; they also transformed her. Just like my daughter's eyeglasses, we need to recognize how the Word of God both transforms us and helps us see.

*Transforming us.* We cannot respond faithfully to God unless God radically rewires our hearts and minds. In fact, part of responding faithfully to God involves allowing God to transform us through his Word.

Listen to what Paul says in Romans 12:2—"Do not conform to the pattern of this world, but be transformed by the renewing of your mind. Then you will be able to test and approve what God's will is—his good, pleasing and perfect will." A few observations. There are two commands in the first half of this verse: "Do not conform" and "be transformed." The first command assumes that the pattern of this world is our default mode. The pattern of this world is like a magnetic force that drags us along. We must not conform to it.

The second command shows us that God calls us to a different direction in life—one that aligns with God's will. The command "be transformed" is passive. This means that transformation comes through something or someone acting on us. If a baseball coach tells a player, "Hit the ball" (active), then the player carries out the action. But if a coach says, "Get hit by the ball" (passive), then the player positions himself to receive the action. In the same way, Paul recognizes that transformation is not something we do to ourselves; instead, someone outside of ourselves transforms us.

There is, however, a role we play. Our transformation takes place "by the renewing of [our] mind." Just like a garden overgrown with weeds needs renewal, so do our minds. This renewal is how we get transformed. How does mind renewal happen? Chiefly through God's Word by the power of the Holy Spirit.

The point here is to recognize that we should be asking, "How might God use this passage to renew my mind and therefore transform me? Who does God want me to be(come)?"

Just think about how God is transforming us through prayerful study and basking in God's presence through passages like Ephesians 2:1-10. God might reorient us to see how our captivity to sin led to death. He redirects our affections toward God's gracious love for us in Christ. Our default is to assume our works put us in right standing with God, but God rewires us to see that "by grace you have been saved, through faith . . . not by works" (Eph 2:8-9). Over time, through the renewal of our minds, we experience transformation; we live into our identity as those who have died, risen, and ascended with Christ.

Consider how God might transform us through putting on the glasses of Psalm 121: "My help comes from the LORD, the Maker of heaven and earth" (Ps 121:1). If our default is to worry and to look to the idols of power, fame, and fortune for help, Psalm 121 molds us to become people who trust in God, the maker of heaven and earth who ever watches over his people.

Consider how God's law at Sinai, the Sermon on the Mount, or the book of Proverbs can form us into wise, virtuous people. Look at how Proverbs opens its book and expresses its aims:

> For gaining wisdom and instruction;
>> for understanding words of insight;
> for receiving instruction in prudent behavior,
>> doing what is right and just and fair (Prov 1:2-3)

These proverbs impart wisdom, cultivate an ability to decipher difficult sayings, and shape us into the sorts of people who live justly.

Listen to how David describes his transformation through God's law.

> The law of the LORD is perfect,
>> refreshing the soul.
> The statutes of the LORD are trustworthy,
>> making wise the simple.
> The precepts of the LORD are right,
>> giving joy to the heart.
> The commands of the LORD are radiant,
>> giving light to the eyes. (Ps 19:7-8)

According to David, God's Word brings refreshment, makes us wise, gives us joy, and gives a spark of life to our eyes.

Willpower is not enough to respond faithfully to God's voice. We need to open ourselves up to God's transformation, to God's ability to rewire our minds and cultivate virtue in us through Scripture. Through this process of continual transformation, we are becoming those who are living faithfully in God's world.

Sometimes we can beat ourselves up if we cannot exactly remember an action step from our morning devotions later in the day. I wonder, however, if the most prominent way we respond faithfully to God's Word is by allowing it to renew our minds and transform us. When we are transformed, then we will be unconsciously responding faithfully to God's Word, for it will flow through everything we do, shaping our intuitions and outlook.

After all, notice the result of being transformed in the second half of Romans 12:2: "Then you will be able to test and approve what God's will is—his good, pleasing and perfect will." Being transformed will enable us to discern God's will as we go about life.

Anna's little pink glasses remind me of my own need for the lenses of Scripture in my life. Those glasses reactivated the eye that would wander slightly. Now, her eyes are in harmony and her vision is correctable to 20/20 vision. Similarly, God's Word transforms our wandering minds, reshapes our desires, and instills within us our identity in Christ. We respond faithfully to God's Word by allowing it to renew our minds. As a result, God transforms us into the sort of people whose entire lives might be said to be a living response to God's Word.

*Seeing well.* God's Word is also like eyeglasses in the sense that it helps us see the world in a new, truer light.

When my brother-in-law was a kid, he'd sit inches away from the TV. His parents never knew why until he saw an eye doctor. Katie (my wife) recalls that when he finally got glasses at age five it was as if he was seeing the world for the first time. He would look around with wonder, amazed at everything he could see. Scripture is similar; it offers us new lenses for seeing and living in God's world. One way we respond faithfully to God's voice is by allowing his Word to be the lens through which we view life.

So the question is, Will I respond to God by allowing his Word to be the lens through which I see life?

Here are a few examples of how Scripture opens up a new vision of the world.

The story of David and Goliath (1 Sam 17) is a favorite among kids. The typical "application" is that we should trust God when we face the Goliaths in our lives. A study of 1 Samuel 17 in its context, however, pushes us away from this sort of moralizing. The four chapters prior to 1 Samuel 17 revolve around why Saul is rejected as king and how God is electing a new king whose heart aligns with God's. The story of David and Goliath introduces us to the sort of king God's people need. David trusts in God and is willing to fight a foe on behalf of the people. David is concerned for the glory of God's name. God acts on behalf of such a king.

A faithful response to 1 Samuel 17 would be to see the world through its lens. Will we see a world in need of a king who trusts God when all other kings fear? Will we long for a king who with God's help defeats the greatest of foes? Sure, we might want to emulate the character of the king, but this is secondary to seeing ourselves as part of a story where we need a king who is far more faithful than we are and who will intervene on our behalf.

As another example, consider Isaiah 1:21-26. This potent poem depicts how Zion has gone from a faithful city to a city full of injustice. God promises, though, to purify his city to be faithful once again. The poem opens with these words:

> See how the faithful city
>    has become a prostitute!
> She once was full of justice,

> righteousness used to dwell in her—
> but now murderers! (Is 1:21)

Ouch! God is calling Zion a "prostitute." This shocking meta-phor is surely intended to disrupt Zion's view of itself. Zion is a prostitute in the sense that its leaders are accepting bribes from the powerful in exchange for ignoring the pleas for justice from the vulnerable orphans and widows (Is 1:23).

What if we were willing to see our responses to cries of injustice through the metaphor of prostitution? What if Isaiah 1:21 helped us see our tendencies to gain and retain power at the expense of advocating for the oppressed? We'd be responding faithfully to God's Word if we did.

As another example, consider Psalm 121. When a child is scared to fall asleep, imagine the new vantage point on God that 121:3-4 offers: "He who watches over you will not slumber; indeed, he who watches over Israel will neither slumber nor sleep." When someone is facing the long journey of cancer treat-ment, a faithful response to Psalm 121 may be to dare to trust the repeated claim that God is keeping watch: "The LORD will watch over your coming and going both now and forevermore" (Ps 121:8). This is not just the power of positive thinking; this is coming to view the world and God as it truly is. Viewing life as unfolding before a faithful God whose gaze is ever on his people.

These are just a few examples of how we can respond faith-fully to God's Word by allowing it to define our vision of reality.

When Anna was two, we visited my parents in Indiana. Our first night there we read the book *The Little Engine That Could*. It tells the story of how the mighty train engines could not pull a container of toys over a steep mountain to deliver them to all of the good boys and girls on the other side. Then a small engine volunteers, to everyone's surprise. The Little Engine kept saying to itself, "I think I can, I think I can, I think I can." With its unbreakable will, the Little Engine eventually made it over the hill and everyone lived happily ever after. After finishing the story, I tucked Anna in and did not think anything more about the story.

The next morning we went swimming. She became scared to jump into the pool and stood on the edge frozen like a statue. I said to Anna, "You've got this!" Then she turned her little hands into fists and said: "I think I can, I think I can, I think I can." A moment later, she plunged right into the pool. The *Little Engine That Could* became a lens for my daughter to see the world in a new light. This is a world where she could do the impossible if she did not give up.

Of course, the orthodoxy of *The Little Engine That Could* is shaky, but it shows how a book can serve as eyeglasses. If the Bible offers us infallible and inspired lenses for seeing the world, then we would be responding faithfully if Scripture became the spectacles through which we view God's world and our place within it.

## CONCLUSION

Step six, building off of step five, brings us to ask, "How might I or we respond faithfully to what God is saying through his Word?" To answer this question, a framework to be mindful of is the dynamic interaction between the Holy Spirit, the Bible, and you in real life. You come as you are to read the Bible and discern what the author would have hoped for in terms of a faithful response from a reader. All the while, the Holy Spirit illuminates your heart to understand the passage, personalizes what God is saying through the Word, and empowers you to faithfully respond in real life.

Lest we think that responding faithfully is all about doing, I went on to show how a faithful response to God's voice includes being and seeing. Adopting the metaphor of glasses, responding faithfully to God's Word means allowing it to renew our minds, thereby transforming us. We must also adopt the Bible's vision of reality as our own lens.

Here are three questions revolving around doing, being, and seeing that might prove useful as you discern what a faithful response entails:

- At the intersection of your real life circumstances and the passage's perlocutionary intent, *what* is the Holy Spirit inviting you to *do*?
- At the intersection of your real life circumstances and the passage's perlocutionary intent, *who* is the Holy Spirit *transforming you into*?
- At the intersection of your real life circumstances and the passage's perlocutionary intent, *how* is the Holy Spirit inviting you to *see*?

Steps five and six aim to encourage us to build our house on the rock by responding faithfully to God's Word.

## DISCUSSION QUESTIONS

1. Recall the three ways the Holy Spirit contributes to Bible reading: illumination, personalization, and transformation.

Can you think of a time when the Holy Spirit spoke to you in a personal way through Scripture?

2. In your own words, how might you explain the difference between "application" and "faithful response"? Is this difference significant for you and for your walk with the Lord? If so, in what ways?

3. Have you ever approached Scripture with the intention of seeking transformation from its words? What might look different if you expected God to change you through studying Scripture?

4. In what ways did you find the "eyeglasses" illustration useful? How might God's Word change us and change the way we see the world? Use Psalm 23 as an example.

# Epilogue

WHILE DEVELOPING THE SIX STEPS, I stumbled on a "Six-Step" dance on YouTube. It is the most basic move in breakdancing. I have always marveled at breakdancers—such agility, rhythm, and style. I'm a stiff, bulky 6'6" dude in his forties. People like me never breakdance. Well, to help me identify with your experience in this book, I tried to learn the breakdance Six-Step with the help of b-boy Vincanity on YouTube.

A few things became clear from my breakdancing attempts. For one, we do not learn to breakdance only by watching and listening. We learn by doing it, repeatedly. In addition, our beginning efforts will be slow and clunky, but, over time, the steps become intuitive and speed increases.

Some toddlers keep on crawling even when they are able to walk. They are confident in their crawl and know they are faster on their hands and knees. This book is an invitation to move from crawling to walking, or from observing to breakdancing. At first, these steps will feel unnatural, slow, and perhaps unproductive. Over time, these moves will become second nature, you'll pick up speed, and the fruits of the approach will become obvious as you study the Bible.

Your experience with this book will be similar to my learning the breakdancing Six-Step. Reading this book will only take you so far. Your growth as an interpreter will only come by trying these steps yourself over and over. As we conclude this journey together, I want to summarize all six steps and then respond to a few practical questions you might be asking.

## THE SIX STEPS

What follows is a brief summary of all six steps. In appendix two you will find a "Six-Step Journal Template" that might prompt your own ideas about how to keep track of the six steps as you study.

*Step one: Posture.* We begin with posture. We need to approach the Bible as children, trusting that God's Word is for our good and seeing our need for "family" in the process of interpretation.

Like Mary who sat at Jesus' feet, we come to Scripture desiring to meet with and learn from God. Here is a prayer that captures this posture: "Our Father, we come as your children. We long to sit at your feet and hear your voice. Send your Holy Spirit that we might savor the Son as we read your word. We are hungry for you. Speak, O Lord. In the name of your Son, Jesus Christ. Amen."

*Step two: Flow.* With a childlike posture, we begin with carefully listening to the passage we are studying. God inspired human authors to communicate through a flow of thought across a passage. Finding the flow of thought involves a grasp of how subunits work together in a passage. Here are the steps for identifying subunits:

- Read the passage through for initial exposure.

- Reread the passage and put slashes (/) where you notice shifts in thought within the passage.

- Mark terms or ideas that repeat across the passage.

- Write titles for each subunit, as this forces you to conceptualize each set of verses and think about how each set relates to the next.

The whole of the passage's flow should be crystalizing in your mind after becoming alert to the subunits. You might even write a summary statement of the entire passage. While you identify subunits or after, read your passage in light of its genre.

- *Narrative* invites attention to plot (especially tension, climax, and resolution) and the role of characters in the story (especially God).

- *Poetry* requires that we be mindful of parallelism, how the thought in one line advances or develops in the next line. We must also ask what the imagery in the passage is trying to help us see.

- *Law* divides into two types—general or case laws—and we must consider what sphere of life the law is addressing.

- *Letters* follow a typical form, so we need to discern what part of the letterform we are reading. Also, the lengthy sentences that unfold within letters require that we identify the main idea of a passage through arrowing.

**Step three: Context.** Having focused in on our passage through a careful reading, it is time to situate the passage within its context. There are two contexts in step three: historical context and book context.

Since God spoke to original audiences in ways that made sense in their times and cultures, we must attend to the historical context of the passage we are studying. Here are three questions to keep in mind:

- *When* is this taking place? (see timelines)
- *Where* is this taking place? (see maps)
- *How* does the passage fit within the culture of the time? (see a study Bible)

Each passage is also set with an unfolding message within a book. The key question when it comes to book context is this:

- *Why* has this passage been included *here* in the book?

In order to answer this question, we would be wise to read the immediately surrounding chapters and to gain a grasp of the whole structure of the book by reading the entire book and with the help of a study Bible or a video from the Bible Project.

***Step four: Whole Bible.*** Steps two and three involve the basics of exegesis—trying to understand what a passage meant in its original context by carefully reading the passage literarily and in its contexts. In step four, we zoom out by asking how a passage points to Jesus and plays a role in the Bible's redemptive story.

We begin this step by pondering how a passage bears witness to Jesus. The most basic way to do this is by looking for parallels. Here is the lead question:

- *What* does this passage say about God, and how is this reflected in Jesus?

Each passage is also part of a larger story of redemptive history that centers on Jesus. God's covenants form the backbone of this story of salvation. Creation and the fall into sin set the stage for God's mission to restore God's ideal of having a people who live before him and experience his blessing in the place God made for them. God's mission of restoration unfolds across his covenants with Abraham, Moses, David, and the new covenant in Jesus that finalize in the new creation.

Once we find where our passage fits within redemptive history, we can surf the wave of redemptive history by seeing how it has been developing, catching it, and riding it through the rest of redemptive history to Jesus' first and second comings.

**Step five: Savor God.** Steps five and six are intentional moments of engaging personally with God in response to everything you have studied. Step five frames communion with God as the pinnacle of reading Scripture.

*Lectio divina* (divine reading) is an ancient approach to reading the Bible that prioritizes meeting with God. It consists of four parts:

- *Lectio* (reading or study) pertains to studying the Bible, as done in steps two through four.
- *Meditatio* (meditation) is the intentional, careful chewing on God's Word.
- *Oratio* (prayer) relates to prayerful engagement with God as we read the Bible.
- *Contemplatio* (contemplation) is when we bask and rest in what God is showing us through the Bible.

By rereading the passage amidst prayerful engagement with God, we push beyond analysis paralysis to a living God who wishes to meet with us through our study.

*Step six: Faithful response.* In step six, we aim for a faithful response to what God is saying to us through the Bible. A faithful response to God's voice will emerge out of the intersection between the Holy Spirit, the Bible, and you in real life. The Holy Spirit will help you understand the Bible, connect this to your own life, and empower you to respond faithfully.

By way of summary, a multifaceted approach is essential for reading the Bible. We begin with a childlike spirit, continue via the flow of the passage, gain clarity through context, consider the larger story that points to Jesus, and culminate by savoring God and responding faithfully to God's voice.

## ADVICE

Questions will naturally arise when you put the six steps into practice. Here are answers to what I anticipate will be the most frequently asked questions.

*What books of the Bible are the best to start with?* Start with the book of the Bible that most excites you. God has been preparing your heart with excitement about a certain book, so why not start there! As a word of caution, however, I would not choose a super difficult book such as Leviticus, Job, Ecclesiastes, Isaiah, or Revelation. These books have less familiar contexts or literary conventions that make them a challenge for beginners.

If you don't have a book you are already excited about, three suggestions come to mind: Genesis, a Gospel (Mark or John), or Philippians. Genesis sets the stage for the entire Bible and is quite accessible due to its compelling narratives, so you can't go wrong starting there. If you want to dive into Jesus' life, Mark is exciting and accessible. As for John, its message is highflying and pushes us beyond the surface level of meaning, yet many testify to being transformed by studying it. If you want to begin with a short letter by Paul, consider Philippians as an option.

*Do you really expect me to go through all six steps every time I read a passage from the Bible?* These six steps are meant to offer a holistic approach to reading the Bible. So, if you want a robust reading of the Bible, then you'll want to be mindful of all six steps. Yet, I am also a realist. A pastor once told our staff repeatedly, "Anything worth doing is worth doing even poorly." For the six steps, I'd say, "Bible study is worth doing even if you cannot perform all six steps." I realize time is limited. Let me give a few bits of advice.

You don't necessarily need to spend the same amount of time on each of the six steps. Usually, step two will require the most time, but you can decide which of the other steps you'll devote more or less attention to. Over time these six steps will become second nature.

Also, you do not need to confine the practice of all six steps to one block of time. Sometimes you can utilize a few steps in the morning and the rest in the evening when reading the same passage. Other times, steps five and six can be an ongoing part of your day, as you meditate on a passage and prayerfully respond. Sometimes you can return to the same passage day after day, applying different steps each day.

Here is what I often do when I don't have enough time to work through all six steps. I offer a brief prayer for illumination (step 1), actively read the passage to detect its flow of thought (step 2), and then prayerfully engage with God to savor who he is (step 5) and listen for how I should respond (step 6).

The six steps are not here to make you feel guilty or avoid Bible reading if you don't have enough time to apply them all. Ideally, you'd apply all six steps, but even using a few will enrich your times of study.

*Can I switch the order of the six steps around?* Yes, indeed! Some will prefer to have a grasp of context (step 3) before they carefully read their passage (step 2). If that's you, by all means please look at context before turning to flow. I prefer to be familiar with a passage before considering context, but I realize others like to have a wider picture in view.

I imagine that breakdancers can improvise and do the steps in various orders or even skip steps at times. Let the six steps be a launching pad toward finding a rhythm and order that works for you.

*How might we use these six steps in a small group setting?* We have developed discussion questions for each step at the end of each chapter. Small groups can easily use these if they choose to read through this book in a group setting.

For small groups that are studying a book of the Bible and want to organize their time around the six steps, here is a possible template:

- Opening: leader reminds the group of the importance of our posture, provides time of quiet, and prays for illumination (step 1)
- Study the passage (steps 2 and 3)
  - Read passage aloud as a group.
  - Individually, carefully read the passage for its flow and flag items in the passage that are confusing or

where you need historical clarification; consider printing out the passage so each individual can easily mark the passage.

- As a group, share observations and questions about the passage. The group leader might have a historically rich study Bible like the *NIV Cultural Backgrounds Study Bible* handy as a reference for questions.

- Jesus and the bigger story (step 4)

  - Group discussion:

    - What does this passage teach about God, and how do we see this in Jesus? What does this passage teach about humanity, and how do we see this in Jesus?

    - Where does this passage fit within redemptive history?

- Response (steps 5 and 6)

  - Individually, read back through the passage savoring God and inviting God to help you see what a faithful response to this passage involves.

  - As a group, share insights from your time of individual reflection.

  - Close in prayer, praising God in light of the passage and calling on God for empowerment to respond faithfully.

***Does this method work if I am reading larger sections of the Bible at a time?*** Most of my advice relates to individual passages (no longer than one chapter), but some of you will be reading through the Bible in a year. To reach that goal you will need to read three chapters per day. So, is it possible to apply the six steps to three chapters at a time?

Yes, but at a bigger picture level. In step two, instead of labeling every subunit, label every chapter instead to discern how each chapter builds on the previous one. In step three, a sense for book context will likely be easier to detect when you are reading larger sections of Scripture. In step four, focus on the major threads across the chapters and how these are pointing to Jesus. In step five, return to meditate on the "white hot" areas of each chapter where you sense God is most powerfully revealing himself or speaking to you. In step six, invite God to clarify how what he is saying either through the whole or through one part of the chapters speaks to your life and respond accordingly.

In my experience as a Bible reader and teacher, those who semi-regularly read the entire Bible will be able to more easily grasp the context of passages (step 3) and how a passage fits into the whole of the Bible (step 4).

***What are the best resources for a new student of the Bible to invest in?*** First, invest in a study Bible. The *NIV Cultural Backgrounds Study Bible* provides helpful historical information. The *Africa Study Bible* is also a great resource for benefiting from an African vantage point. Since readers from various cultures might miss different elements in the text, it is valuable to have resources from multiple cultural perspectives. The more general NIV and ESV Study Bibles are solid resources too.

Second, a one-volume Bible commentary can come in handy, especially when reading tricky passages. The *Africa Bible*

*Commentary* (Zondervan, 2010) provides comments on every chapter of the Bible by African Bible scholars. They are currently working on a second edition that will incorporate more of an African perspective. The *South Asia Bible Commentary* (Zondervan, 2015) offers insights into all books of the Bible from south Asian Bible scholars. I often recommend the *New Bible Commentary*, 21st Century Edition (InterVarsity Press, 1994). Having one of these handy will be useful. Some people like having concordances on hand too, but the word search capabilities available through StepBible.org make hard copy concordances less necessary (see appendix 1 on word studies).

## FINAL WORD

Blessed is the one . . . whose delight is in the law of the LORD,
    and who meditates on his law day and night.
That person is like a tree planted by streams of water,
    which yields its fruit in season. (Ps 1:1-3)

While in Israel, the words of Psalm 1:3 came to life for me. We were hiking along a canyon near the Dead Sea. A dry riverbed was our guide. All around were whitish-tan walls of arid rock and sand. There was no vegetation in sight.

As we rounded a bend, a tree with bright green leaves popped into view. Like a diamond amidst coal, the green tree sparkled with life amid its barren surroundings. The reason: a small pool of water.

When we delight in and meditate on God's Word, water begins to flow. Our roots sink deep into the life of God and life springs forth in lifeless situations.

Hundreds of years after Psalm 1 was written, an African bishop in the fourth century AD named Athanasius famously speaks of Scripture as water for the thirsty. After listing the books in the Bible, he states, "These are fountains of salvation, that they who thirst may be satisfied with the living words they contain."[1] Like fountains that satisfy the thirsty, the books of the Bible remain active, bringing life to the thirstiest of souls. Countless generations of Christians have experienced this.

So, as we close, let us ask again, "Why study the Bible?" At least for me, it is not merely because the Bible is a remarkable historical and literary artifact, although it certainly is. Not merely because it is the bestselling book of all time. Not merely so we can be gurus that draw principles from it for success today. Not even because we want to "know our Bible better." We study the Bible to meet with the living God. We study to find refreshment for our thirsty souls from the living waters of Christ. We study so that our roots sink deep. We study so that God can transform us so that we bear fruit for the good of the world and to the glory of God. May this book help direct you to meet with and be transformed by the living God as you study his living and active Word.

## DISCUSSION QUESTIONS

1. How has your vision for how to read the Bible changed as a result of this book?

2. What steps are you most excited about trying to implement? Why?

---

[1] Athanasius, "Festal Letter XXXIX," NPNF[2] 4:1327.

3. What book of the Bible are you going to spend time studying next? Is there anyone that can partner with you in the journey?

4. As you consider changes in how you read the Bible, what do you think will be the greatest challenge?

Appendix 1

# Word Study

OVER THE COURSE OF STUDYING THE BIBLE, we will see words that repeat or are confusing and we will want to better understand those words. I have chosen to not emphasize word studies in this book because it is easy to miss the mark and import too much meaning or the wrong meanings into a single word. My conviction is that beginners are best served by focusing on the flow of thought across a passage (step 2) rather than focusing myopically on a single word. For those who wish to dip their toes into the waters of word studies, here is some practical advice.

*Why do a word study?* In our native languages, we do not need to do word studies. We know what a word means already when we hear it in its context. As soon as we enter a new culture, though, we are often unaware of the nuances of certain words.

For example, when we lived in Australia, a colleague said, "This year's new students are pretty *ordinary*." In America, *ordinary* is a neutral term, so I initially took the statement to mean the group of students is academically where one would expect in a given year. But as my colleague kept talking I realized *ordinary* meant something quite different. In Australia, *ordinary* can have a negative connotation in certain uses, meaning mediocre or something of the sort. Once I became aware of how *ordinary* can mean various things depending on usage in Australia, I could better understand what someone meant when using the term in similar contexts.

When it comes to the Bible, most of us read a translation in our own native language. Since we are reading words we are familiar with in our own language, it is easy to forget that we are reading a translation from Hebrew, Greek, and Aramaic. We often assume that whatever a word means in our culture must mean the same thing for authors of the Bible. But there may be nuances of a word in the original language that differ from how I would use an English equivalent today. A word study helps us become aware of those different meanings.

***What is a word study?*** A word study examines the uses of a Hebrew, Aramaic, or Greek word in order to better grasp the range of ideas (connotations) that the word may convey. For example, imagine that you are studying Exodus 33 and Exodus 33:18 catches your attention: "Then Moses said, 'Now show me your glory.'" Let's say you want to do a word study on *glory* from this passage. In order to do so, you would look up all of the uses of *glory* (*kābôd*) in Hebrew to become alert to the range of ideas that may relate to this term. The easiest way to get a list of such verses is by using stepbible.org. If you pull up Exodus 33:18 there, you can click on the word *glory*. It will then provide a definition of the term and give you the option to click a link to view all of its occurrences.

Consider the following sentences where *glory* occurs:

Moses could not enter the tent of meeting because the cloud had settled on it, and the *glory* of the LORD filled the tabernacle. (Ex 40:35)

How long will you people turn my *glory* into shame? (Ps 4:2)

A look at these sentences shows different nuances accompanying the term *glory*.

In the first sentence (Ex 40:35), glory is a divine quality ("of the LORD"). God's glory parallels "the cloud," so references to God's glory may call to mind a tangible representation of it in the form of a cloud. Also, God's glory seems to prevent human access to the tabernacle.

In the second sentence (Ps 4:2), David is speaking about his own, human glory: "my glory." Since it contrasts "shame," it is apparent that there is a social dimension to glory relating to honor. Glory in this verse is fragile, for adversaries can dishonor David resulting in his public shame.

By simply comparing these two occasions where *glory* occurs, we already see a range of ideas that can relate to *kābôd*: divine and human, public honor rather than shame, visible via a cloud, and separating God from people. Now, imagine how the range of ideas would expand if we considered all two hundred times the Hebrew term for glory (*kābôd*) occurs!

A word study, however, is not done after collating all the different ideas that may inform uses of "glory" (*kābôd*). The next step is to return to the passage you are studying, in our case Exodus 33:18, and consider what *glory* conveys within the flow of the passage.

There are several dangers at this point, particularly an illegitimate totality transfer. Many are tempted to transfer all of the possible nuances of an original language term back into its use in a particular verse. In other words, we make the mistake of assuming that a word will always mean everything it can possibly mean every time it occurs. This does not make sense in any language. For instance, compare the following sentences from the English language:

The *word* on the street is that Subway is going out of business.

Write down the *word* you see on the screen.

To start my day, I like to spend time in the *Word*.

People would think you were crazy if you imposed the third use of *word* on the first and said, "Since *word* refers to God's Word in the Bible, then you must mean by 'the *word* on the street' that it is a true, divine message that you have heard." Or imagine that you imposed the meaning of the second on the third and said, "Since *word* is singular rather than *words* (plural), then you must like to start your day in a single word." Of course, this approach to words would be nonsense in English, but for some reason we think it is different when we are dealing with biblical languages.

As we return to what glory contributes to the meaning of "Now, show me your glory" (Ex 33:18), a process of discernment begins that leans heavily on reading Exodus 33:18 within its context. You'd be asking, "Within the flow of thought in this particular passage, what is *glory* most likely conveying in verse 18?"

There are two hundred occurrences of *kābôd* in the Old Testament, so I cannot show all of my work here. In practice, I would lean most heavily on the eleven occurrences of this term in the book of Exodus. Two occurrences describe the "glory and beauty" of Aaron's priestly garments (Ex 28:2, 40)—since these refer to the human realm, the other uses are more relevant. In almost all of the other uses in Exodus, *glory* is closely connected to the "cloud" by which God makes his presence known (Ex 16:7-10; 24:16-17; 40:34, 35). So, Moses' request, "Show me your glory," is a desire to see a tangible expression of God's glory manifest through the cloud. This line of thinking is confirmed when reading Exodus 33–34, for we are told "the LORD came down in the cloud" in Exodus 34:5. Thus, a word study of *glory* helps us see that Moses is requesting God's appearance in a cloud. Moses is not asking for a heavenly vision of God's glory. Moses is seeking a tangible experience of God's presence, as he needs assurance that God will remain with Moses and Israel after an incident of grievous sin.

*The goal of a word study.* When performing a word study, we must keep our goal in mind—to discern what the word is conveying within the flow of thought of a particular passage. The goal is *not* to offer a new translation; let's be modest about our linguistic capabilities. The goal is *not* to impose all possible meanings of a word into the use of the word in your passage (remember the *illegitimate totality transfer*). Your goal is simply to become alert to what the word in view is conveying within the flow of the text.

*Steps in a productive word study.*

1.  Select a word in the original language in your passage.

    Since most people do not know Hebrew, Aramaic, or Greek, you need assistance in discovering what the word is in Hebrew (the Old Testament), Aramaic (parts of Daniel and Ezra), or Greek (the New Testament). The best online resource for this is stepbible.org. Bring up your passage and then hover your cursor over the word in your verse (*glory* in Ex 33:18). Left-click on the term and you will see the word and a definition appear in a new pane. In the new pane, click on the number next to where it says "occurs in the Bible." This will bring up all of the verses where the term occurs in the main pane. You can also use concordances available online to identify the other uses of your term. If your word has too many occurrences, consider a combination of words from your verse (*show* and *glory*) or limit the search to a particular corpus (only Exodus or only the Pentateuch).

2. Examine all uses of the word in their literary contexts

   ▪ Start with uses of the word in the same *book* or works in the same *section* (Torah, Letters, Gospels). Categorize according to use and ideas conveyed, as we began to do with Exodus above.

   ▪ Consider uses of the term from the same *genre*. Categorize according to use and ideas conveyed.

   ▪ Consider all other uses of that term elsewhere *in that testament*. Continue to classify recurring patterns of ideas.

3. Compare your different findings from the book, genre, and testament levels. Any insights emerging about its particular use in your passage?

4. Reexamine how your term is contributing to the message of your passage through a close reading. Here you will

identify what your word is conveying and thereby contributing to the passage. Make sure your sense of the word's meaning is not out of step with the general meaning of the passage. If you can find similar uses of the term in the same book of the Bible or same section, then you can have more confidence in your conclusions.

As a final word of caution, do not build a Bible study or a sermon around a single word study. You would be on firmer ground if you let the overall message of the passage guide your study, with insights from a word study merely supplementing along the way.

# Appendix 2

# Six-Step Journal Template

| Step 1: Posture *Our Father, we come as your children. We long to sit at your feet and hear your voice. Send your Holy Spirit that we might savor the Son as we read your Word. We are hungry for you. Speak, O Lord. In the name of your Son, Jesus Christ. Amen.* | |
|---|---|
| **Step 2: Flow** <br> *Titles for Subunits* <br> I. <br> II. <br> III. <br> etc. | *Genre Insights* (plot, parallelism, etc.) |
| **Step 3: Context** <br> *Historical Context* <br> *When is this taking place?* <br><br> *Where is this taking place?* <br><br> *How does the passage fit within the culture of the time?* | *Book Context* <br> *Why is the passage included here in the book?* |
| **Step 4: Whole Bible** <br> *What does this passage say about God, and how is this reflected in Jesus?* <br><br> *How does this fit within God's big story of redemption that centers on Jesus' first and second comings?* | |
| **Step 5: Savor God** <br> Pray, meditate, contemplate. <br><br> Reflections: | **Step 6: Faithful Response** <br> How is God speaking through the passage to you in real life? What would a faithful response look like? |

# Scripture Index